# WINE DOGS

## DELUXE EDITION

*the dogs of Australasian wineries*

Proudly in partnership with

*for Tok, Tarka and Stella*

# FOREWORD

*by Huon Hooke*

**just as** *every barn and bakery has a resident cat, every winery seems to have a dog. While the cats have a purpose – keeping down the mouse population – winery dogs fill a less-easily defined role. Is it to keep the winemaker company when no-one else will? (We all know wine people can be notoriously one-track, to the point where no normal people want to have anything to do with them!) Or is it that well-known medical side-benefit of owning a pet – that nursing, caressing or playing with a pet lowers the pulse-rate and counteracts stress? (Especially useful during vintage.) Or do dogs perform some other clandestine function that the wine industry is furtively keeping secret from the rest of us? Are dogs the real palate-power behind the skilled business of making wine? We know their sense of smell and taste is many times keener than that of humans.*

*That must be it! When no-one is looking, Rover dons a white coat and is up on his hind legs, in the lab, doing the blending trials. While his owner is doing what he really enjoys most – heading down to the pub to sink a few schooners with his mates, or spoiling a good walk by bashing a small white ball around a paddock – the dog is putting in where it really counts.*

*I've long harboured this suspicion about winery dogs. I mean, does Vanya Cullen really think we believe SHE makes those heavenly cabernet merlots? It's Rosie and Pookie the labradors who've always been the brains behind the place. Len Evans has his dachshunds, Charlie Melton has his dalmatian, Dan Dineen has the legendary Maynard (was there ever a more famous winery woofer?) and Tim Adams has that playful pair of pooches, Solomon and Fronti. Even John Middleton at Mount Mary has dogs: as far as*

*I know he was the first of a long line of winemakers to have white and black labradors named Chardonnay and Pinot. I wonder if David Hohnen has a Zin? And does Chris Killeen's dog make a sound more like 'Du-riff, du-riff!' than 'Woof, woof'?*

*Winery dogs are important. Fox Creek has – not a pet Reynard – but a border collie called Shadow, who so impressed everyone with his vineyard antics that his owners named a wine after him: Shadow's Run. Yalumba had a famous series of collectable 'horse ports' named after racehorses (Kingston Town, Dulcify, et al.): why not a series of dog ports?*

*Winery dogs are so important in Tasmania (where they have more three-dog nights than most wine regions), that that colourful chronicler of Tassie wineries, Phil Laing, gives a special mention to all winery dogs in his guide,* Tasmanian Wineries. *And along with his obligatory annual prizes for 'best pinot noir', 'best riesling', etc., he also gives a winery dog of the year award. There should be more recognition like this for the winemaker's best friend.*

*Perhaps the most memorable meeting I ever had with a winery dog was on my first visit to Bordeaux in the early 1980s. I'd parked my rented Ford Fiesta at Chateau Ducru-Beaucaillou, and proceeded to stroll at a leisurely pace across the gravel towards what I took to be the main entrance, like any unsuspecting visitor might. A well-groomed man in a sports coat and cravat appeared at the other end of the yard, and proceeded in my direction, evidently intending to greet me. I took him to be the owner, Jean-Eugene Borie. Indeed, I recognised him from photographs. As the gap between us closed he greeted me and I him, and we each extended our hands for the customary shake. As our hands met and clasped, a streak of lightning came from somewhere beyond my field of vision and seemingly in a single bound the creature was upon us, ears flattened against its head by the slipstream, its long legs scarcely in contact with the earth. In a flash its massive jaws snapped shut and its gleaming fangs* clamped onto my hand like a dingo trap. The dog's big mistake was that it had also chomped the hand that fed it, that of Monsieur Borie. I could only assume the lanky young Doberman was trying to protect its master. Dogs can do surprising things, but I have seldom been so surprised by one.

Monsieur Borie laughed it off with some typically French comment about 'un chien méchant' and proceeded to the winery with pipette and tasting glasses as though nothing had happened. I've always been amused by that phrase: instead of the English warning of a dangerous or fierce dog, the French use 'chien méchant', which can mean a malicious dog or just a naughty dog, depending on your frame of mind.

The dogs in this book were well behaved, on the whole. Surprisingly, Craig McGill was set upon by more than one of the hounds herein, while helping the photographer do his job. And he has the scars to prove it. Happy snapping became just plain snapping. Surprising, because Craig and his partner Susan are great dog lovers, and the devoted owners of a number of beautiful huskies. The daddy of the pack is Tok – no doubt short for Tokay.

I applaud Craig and Sue's effort to put dogs in their rightful place, because we all know that behind every successful winemaker there sits a faithful bow-wow. It's a blatant case of the tail wagging the dog, because we all know the dog deserves the lion's share of the credit. So, this is an attempt to right an injustice; to settle an old score and give winery dogs their day. Paws for thought.

HUON HOOKE IS A LEADING AUSTRALIAN WINE WRITER, JUDGE AND EDUCATOR. HE WRITES WEEKLY COLUMNS IN *THE SYDNEY MORNING HERALD 'GOOD LIVING'* AND *GOOD WEEKEND*. HIS ARTICLES APPEAR IN NUMEROUS PUBLICATIONS INCLUDING *AUSTRALIAN GOURMET TRAVELLER WINE, UNCORKED, SLOW WINE* AND *DECANTER*. HE IS A DEVOUT CAT LOVER.

*" Yesterday, I was a dog.*

*Today, I am a dog.*

*Tomorrow, I will probably be a dog.*

*There's just so little hope of advancement."*

———————————— **SNOOPY**

PET HATE: BROCCOLI
OBSESSION: RABBITS
NAUGHTIEST DEED: CHASING THE CHOOKS
FASTEST MEAL CONSUMED: CHICKEN WING
FAVOURITE PASTIME: SLEEP

BETSY

OWNER: OLIVER CRAWFORD | COCKER SPANIEL, 3 | **MAGILL ESTATE** MAGILL, SA

KNOWN ACCOMPLICE: BELLA
OBSESSION: CHASING PARIS THE CAT
NAUGHTIEST DEED: SNEAKING INTO THE FRIDGE AT NIGHT
PET HATE: GETTING UP IN THE MORNING
FAVOURITE TOY: COOKIE MONSTER
FAVOURITE PASTIME: ANYTHING HE'S NOT ALLOWED TO DO
FASTEST MEAL CONSUMED: DINNER FOR FOUR, INCLUDING THE SALAD

OWNER: JOSH SCOTT | JACK RUSSELL TERRIER, 2 | **ALLAN SCOTT WINES** BLENHEIM, NZ

ALLIE

OBSESSION: FOOD
KNOWN ACCOMPLICE: ABBIE
FAVOURITE PASTIME: BASKING IN THE SUN
FAVOURITE TOY: DOES NOT HAVE ONE AT THE MOMENT

**HENKELL VINEYARDS** DIXONS CREEK, VIC | PUG, 1 | OWNER: PETRA HENKELL

## MOLLY

*PET HATE: CATS*
*FAVOURITE TOY: KID'S TOY TEDDY*
*FASTEST MEAL CONSUMED: PRIME MINCE*

**CINDY**

PET HATE: *BEING WASHED*
KNOWN ACCOMPLICE: *CANDY*
FAVOURITE PASTIME: *SLEEPING*
NAUGHTIEST DEED: *ATE THREE PAIRS OF RELATIVES' SANDALS*

**GREVILLEA ESTATE** BEGA, NSW | BEAGLE, 4 | OWNER: WAYNE LUCAS

**OSCAR**

OBSESSIONS: STICKS AND CHILDREN'S TOYS
NAUGHTIEST DEED: CHASING SHEEP
PET HATES: BEING WASHED AND BEING LEFT BEHIND FOR THE DAY
KNOWN ACCOMPLICES: TOM, JAMES JUNIOR AND HARRY
FAVOURITE PASTIME: PRETENDING TO SLEEP WHILE ACTUALLY WATCHING THE DUCKS

**DOMAINE CHANDON** COLDSTREAM, VIC | GERMAN SHORT-HAIRED POINTER, 7 | OWNERS: JAMES AND SALLY GOSPER

PET HATE: THE CAT
OBSESSION: MURDERING SOCCER BALLS
NAUGHTIEST DEED: TO BE ANNOUNCED!
FAVOURITE TOY: SOCCER BALL

16   **FROMM WINERY** BLENHEIM, NZ | BORDER COLLIE X, 7 WEEKS | OWNERS: HATSCH AND SIMON KALBERER, LAVINIA HIROK

**THOMAS**

NAUGHTIEST DEED: DOING
NUMBER 2 IN THE OFFICE
PET HATE: BEING REMINDED
OF THE OFFICE INCIDENT
FAVOURITE PASTIME: LOOKING NERVOUS
FAVOURITE TOY: GERALD THE PRODUCTION MANAGER
OBSESSIONS: BLOWFLIES AND ELECTRIC BLANKETS

**KATO**

OBSESSIONS: FOOD, POLISHING SHOES
NAUGHTIEST DEED: BRINGING HOME DEAD RABBITS AND ROOS
PET HATES: BEING LEFT ALONE, GUNS, GAS GUNS AND LIGHTNING
FASTEST MEAL CONSUMED: CHOOK FOOD
KNOWN ACCOMPLICE: MR BEAN

**MOUNT BROKE WINES** BROKE, NSW | BORDER COLLIE X, 9 AND KATE, 4 | OWNERS: PHIL AND JO McNAMARA

GETTING KATO TO SIT WAS QUITE A PROBLEM BUT MR BEAN WAS MORE RESPONSIVE. UNFORTUNATELY,

EANIE ONLY HAD THREE LEGS AND FELL OVER EVERY TIME HE SAT DOWN. THE FRUSTRATION WAS ALMOST TOO

MUCH FOR KATE. "HOW LONG DOES IT TAKE TO GET A PHOTO? YOU BOYS AREN'T VERY GOOD AT THIS!"

FAVOURITE MOVIE: LADY AND THE TRAMP
KNOWN ACCOMPLICES: MILLY AND MISSY THE CATS
FAVOURITE PASTIMES: BEING CUDDLED AND NOSING PEOPLE IN THE CROTCH
OBSESSION: BARKING AT HEDGEHOGS IN THE MIDDLE OF THE NIGHT
PET HATE: PEAS – WILL SHOOT THEM OUT HER MOUTH WHEN EATING LEFTOVER FOOD

**NEUDORF VINEYARDS** NELSON, NZ | BEARDED COLLIE X, 10 | OWNERS: THE FINN FAMILY

PET HATE: *UNFAMILIAR NOISES*
OBSESSION: *GETTING AS CLOSE TO A LOVED ONE AS POSSIBLE*
NAUGHTIEST DEED: *RUNNING AWAY WITH HER MUM*
FASTEST MEAL CONSUMED: *BREAKFAST*
KNOWN ACCOMPLICES: *OSCAR, LIBBY AND TYSON*
FAVOURITE PASTIME: *GOING TO THE BEACH*

OWNERS: *TREVOR AND ROBYN BOLITHO* | BOXER, 5 | **WAIMEA ESTATES** *NELSON, NZ*

MAYNARD

PET HATE: ALL OTHER PETS
OBSESSIONS: BALLS, WHEELS AND DELIVERY MEN'S HEELS
FAVOURITE PASTIME: FARTING UNDER THE COVERS
NAUGHTIEST DEED: BITING LEN EVANS AND ROLLING A CAR (NOT HIS FAULT)

**TOWER ESTATE** POKOLBIN, NSW | BLUE HEELER, 10 | OWNER: DAN DINEEN

OBSESSION: BARKING AT KIDS ON TRAMPOLINES
NAUGHTIEST DEED: SLEEPING ON THE WINEMAKER'S NEW BED
FAVOURITE TOY: OLIVER'S FOOTBALL
KNOWN ACCOMPLICE: MOLLY
FAVOURITE PASTIMES: SOCIALISING AND SUNBAKING

PATSY

OWNER: GAVIN BERRY | STAFFORDSHIRE X, 8 | **WEST CAPE HOWE** DENMARK, WA

**GEORGE**

OBSESSION: BEING THE PERFECT DOG
NAUGHTIEST DEED: HE'S THE PERFECT DOG
PET HATE: BEING BY HIMSELF
FAVOURITE TOY: PIGGY
KNOWN ACCOMPLICE: MURPHY
FAVOURITE PASTIME: BEING THE PERFECT DOG

**MURPHY**

KNOWN ACCOMPLICE: GEORGE
OBSESSIONS: GUINEA PIGS AND FULL MOONS
NAUGHTIEST DEED: EATING OUR NEIGHBOUR'S GUINEA PIGS
FASTEST MEAL CONSUMED: NEIGHBOUR'S GUINEA PIGS
FAVOURITE PASTIME: BEING A FREE SPIRIT

**DEAKIN ESTATE** IRAAK, VIC | LABRADOR, 9 (TOP) & GOLDEN RETRIEVER, 4 | OWNER: BRIAN FALKENBERG

OBSESSION: CHASING WILD CATS AND RABBITS
NAUGHTIEST DEED: HELPING HERSELF TO BBQ SAUSAGES
PET HATE: PEOPLE WHO IGNORE HER
FAVOURITE TOYS: STUFFED RABBIT AND A SQUASH BALL
FASTEST MEAL CONSUMED: STOLEN BBQ SAUSAGES
KNOWN ACCOMPLICE: HER BROTHER CHOPIN
FAVOURITE PASTIME: SLEEPING IN THE UTE

BLISS

OWNER: GEOFF MATTHEWS | GERMAN SHORT-HAIRED POINTER, 11 | **WITHER HILLS VINEYARDS** BLENHEIM, NZ | 25

**SABI (AKA 'THE ALIEN')**

KNOWN ACCOMPLICE: STELLA
OBSESSIONS: FOOD, ESCAPING AND HIS LOOKS
PET HATE: BEING MISTAKEN FOR A KANGAROO
NAUGHTIEST DEED: EATING BRAS OFF THE CLOTHESLINE
FASTEST MEAL CONSUMED: SIZE 18 CHICKEN IN ONE GULP
FAVOURITE PASTIMES: SUNBAKING AND ACTING STRANGELY

**beam me up, scotty!** *When Voyager Estate wanted their woofer featured in* Wine Dogs *I was physically shaken. These people from the Margaret River seemed pleasant enough but with a dog called 'The Alien', I was worried. What was this dog like? Half machine, half dog? Green with large razor blades for teeth? I was scared and immediately packed an extra pair of pants – but was this enough? Should I pack the whole body armour as well?*

*Well, much to my surprise (and relief), 'The Alien' revealed itself as a truly goofy and friendly Rhodesian ridgeback capable of only putting a smile on everyone's dial. I must admit though, those antennas on the back of his head are a bit of a worry.*

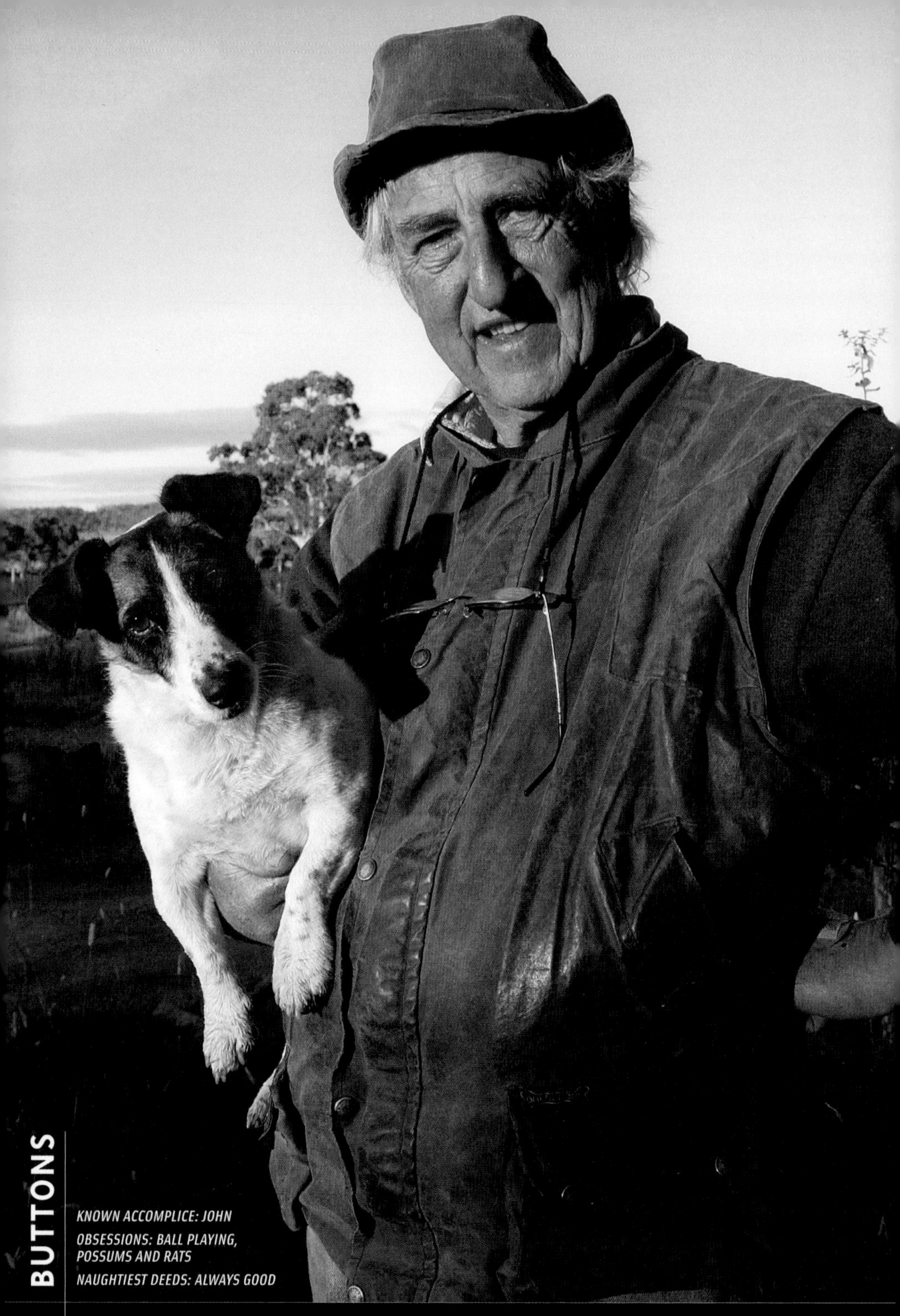

# BUTTONS

*KNOWN ACCOMPLICE: JOHN*

*OBSESSIONS: BALL PLAYING, POSSUMS AND RATS*

*NAUGHTIEST DEEDS: ALWAYS GOOD*



**CRAIGIE KNOWE VINEYARD** *CRANBROOK, TAS* | *JACK RUSSELL TERRIER, 6* | *OWNER: JOHN AUSTWICK (PICTURED*

FAVOURITE TOY: BALL
PET HATE: NO BALL TO PLAY WITH
FAVOURITE PASTIME: BALL PLAYING
GREATEST ACHIEVEMENT: SCORING 38 POINTS ON A SINGLE WORD IN SCRABBLE

BUTTONS

**HUXLEY**

PET HATE: CATS
FAVOURITE TOY: FOOTBALL
KNOWN ACCOMPLICE: WANDOO
FAVOURITE PASTIME: SLEEPING
OBSESSIONS: SOCKS AND SLIPPERS
FASTEST MEAL CONSUMED: ROAST CHICKEN
NAUGHTIEST DEED: SLOBBERING ON CELLAR DOOR STAFF

**HAREWOOD ESTATE** DENMARK, WA | NEAPOLITAN MASTIFF, 8 MONTHS | OWNER: JAMES KELLIE

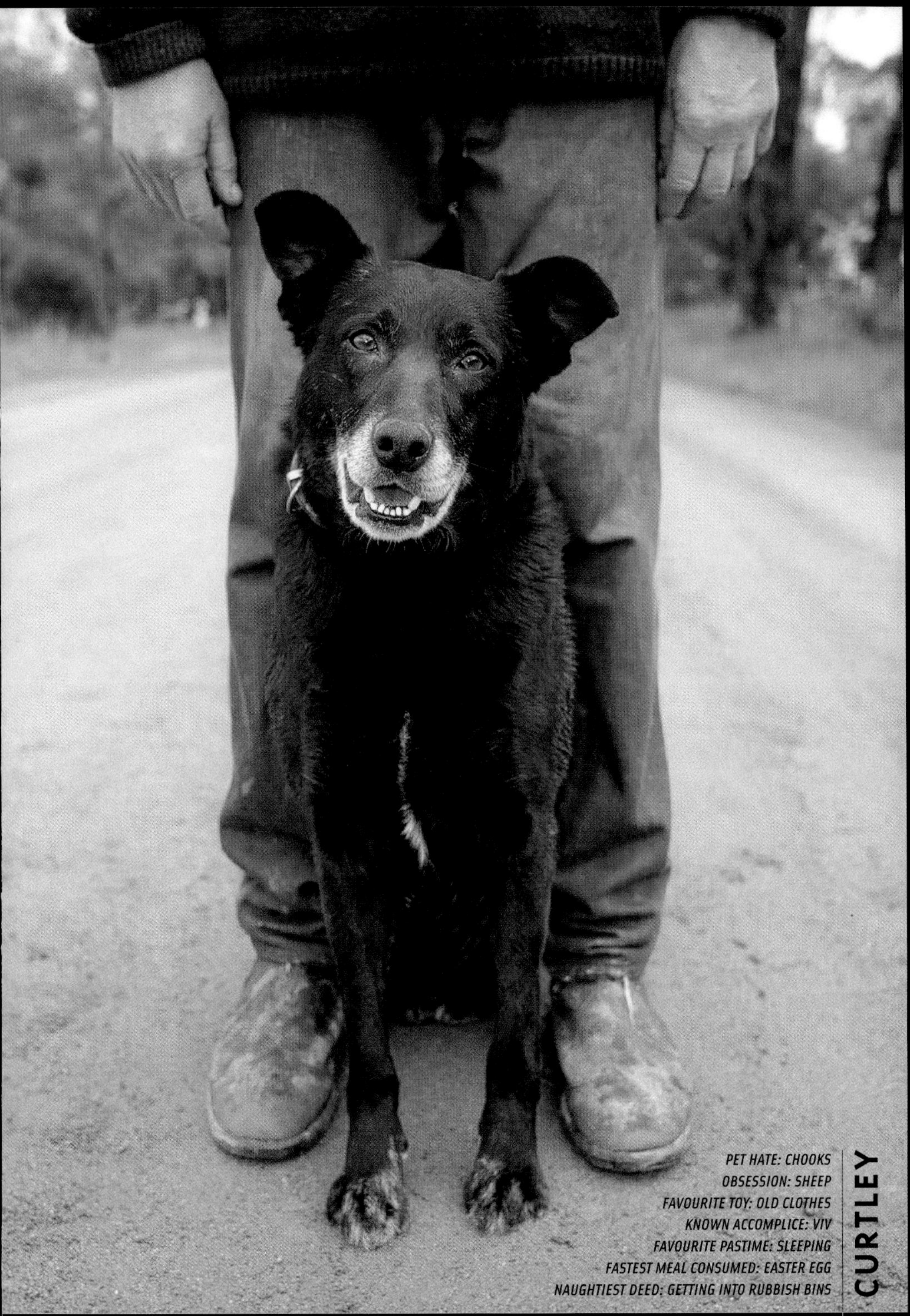

# CURTLEY

PET HATE: CHOOKS
OBSESSION: SHEEP
FAVOURITE TOY: OLD CLOTHES
KNOWN ACCOMPLICE: VIV
FAVOURITE PASTIME: SLEEPING
FASTEST MEAL CONSUMED: EASTER EGG
NAUGHTIEST DEED: GETTING INTO RUBBISH BINS

OWNERS: JIM AND BEV GILBERT | KELPIE, 7 | **GILBERT WINES** KENDENUP, WA

NAUGHTIEST DEED: CHASING FRIENDS' CHICKENS
FAVOURITE TOY: MONTY THE SQUEAKING GORILLA
FASTEST MEAL CONSUMED: ICE CREAM
KNOWN ACCOMPLICES: PIPPIN AND McTAVISH
FAVOURITE PASTIME: SCARING BIRDS
OBSESSION: PINCHING SOFT TOYS FROM NEIGHBOURHOOD CHILDREN

**MUDHOUSE WINES** RENWICK, NZ | AIREDALE TERRIER, 18 MONTHS | OWNER: JENNIFER JOSLIN

OBSESSION: PINECONES
FAVOURITE TOY: OLD SHEEP SKULL
KNOWN ACCOMPLICES: FIN AND BRUNO
FAVOURITE PASTIME: WAITING FOR ACTION
FASTEST MEAL CONSUMED: SANDWICHES – WRAPPER AND ALL
NAUGHTIEST DEED: STEALING LUNCHES FROM THE SMOKO ROOM

POPPY

PET HATE: HOT AIR BALLOONS
OBSESSIONS: CHASING FOXES AND RABBITS
NAUGHTIEST DEED: CARTING SOCKS AND BOOTS TO BED
FASTEST MEAL CONSUMED: THE CAT'S FOOD
KNOWN ACCOMPLICES: ZAC AND STORM
FAVOURITE PASTIME: SLEEPING IN FRONT OF THE UTE

**BROCKVILLE** IRYMPLE, VIC | WHIPPET, 6 | OWNERS: MARK AND LEIGH BOWRING

FAVOURITE TOY: ANYTHING THAT SQUEAKS
PET HATE: OUR NEIGHBOUR GRAHAM CROFT
FAVOURITE PASTIME: RUNNING TO THE VINEYARD
OBSESSION: BOTTOMS OF LARGE
MIDDLE-AGED WOMEN IN TIGHT TROUSERS
NAUGHTIEST DEED: BITING FIVE OF THE
ABOVE DURING HER ADOLESCENCE

RIEUSSEC

TANGO

OBSESSION: LEAPING AND SUSPENDING HERSELF IN MID-AIR
WITH TEETH FIRMLY GRIPPED AROUND A HAND-HELD BALL
PET HATE: NON-PAYING CUSTOMERS
FAVOURITE TOY: ANY BALL OR STICK
FAVOURITE POSITION: LYING IN FRONT OF A WARM FIRE

**BARNADOWN RUN** TOOLLEEN, VIC | MINIATURE FOX TERRIER, 5 | OWNER: ANDREW MILLIS

FASTEST MEAL CONSUMED: A MOUSE
NAUGHTIEST DEED: BECOMING PREGNANT
KNOWN ACCOMPLICES: EWAN McROBERT AND JEFF
FAVOURITE PASTIME: DIGGING OUT MOUSE HOLES

**JADE**

PET HATE: WINE TASTING
FAVOURITE TOY: ANY SOFT STUFFED TOY
FASTEST MEAL CONSUMED: SUSHI
KNOWN ACCOMPLICES: RATS AND BULL
OBSESSIONS: RUNNING AND WALKIES
NAUGHTIEST DEED: SHAKING HERSELF INSIDE AFTER A ROLL IN THE MUD
FAVOURITE PASTIME: PERFORMING ON TOP OF THE PICNIC TABLES

**THE GURDIES WINERY** THE GURDIES, VIC | LABRADOR, 5 | OWNER: YOLANDA KOZIK

KNOWN ACCOMPLICE: OSCAR THE CAT
FAVOURITE TOY: TOY MOUSE THAT VIBRATES
OBSESSION: JUMPING UP AND DOWN LIKE A YO-YO,
PET HATE: BEING A BIG DOG IN A SMALL DOG'S BODY
FAVOURITE PASTIME: CHASING OR BEING CHASED BY OSCAR
NAUGHTIEST DEED: PEEING ON A CARTON OF LAURIENT PERRIER

BASIL

OWNERS: RICHARD ROBSON AND SALLY MARDEN | JACK RUSSELL TERRIER, 6 | **PLANTAGENET WINES** MT BARKER, WA | 39

OBSESSION: COLLECTING CORKS
NAUGHTIEST DEED: BREAKING HIS LEG
FAVOURITE TOYS: A PURPLE BEAR AND 'GORILLA LEGS'
KNOWN ACCOMPLICE: BEAVER THE BOXER
FAVOURITE PASTIME: GOING ANYWHERE IN THE CAR
PET HATES: TRAILERS ATTACHED TO VEHICLES, UMBRELLAS AND RAINCOATS

WAIMEA ESTATES NELSON, NZ | ROUGH COATED JACK RUSSELL TERRIER, 2 | OWNERS: BEN AND ANNA BOLITHO

PET HATES: SHEEP AND COWS
FAVOURITE TOY: THE CAT'S BOWL
KNOWN ACCOMPLICE: MISSY THE CAT
FAVOURITE PASTIME: LYING IN THE SUN
OBSESSION: SITTING IN THE BACK OF UTES
FASTEST MEAL CONSUMED: STEAK OFF THE BBQ
NAUGHTIEST DEED: 5-LITRE URINATION ON THE CARPET

OWNERS: KEVIN AND KIMBERLEY JUDD | BORDER COLLIE X, 14 | CLOUDY BAY, BLENHEIM, NZ | 41

PET HATES: DIESEL TRUCKS, DON
OBSESSION: EATING CHEESE WITH THE OLD BOY ON A THURSDAY ARVO
NAUGHTIEST DEED: EATING OUT OF THE BIN WHEN NOBODY IS HOME
FAVOURITE PASTIME: DOING THE WINERY TOUR WITH MURRAY AT 1.30

**TYRRELL'S VINEYARDS** POKOLBIN, NSW | *STUMPY-TAILED SMITHFIELD, 10* | OWNER: JOHN TYRRELL

SPOT

FASTEST MEAL CONSUMED: TIN OF PAL
FAVOURITE TOY: BUNG OUT OF THE BARREL
KNOWN ACCOMPLICE: CHAMPAGNE THE CAT

BRONSON

OBSESSION: BACK SEAT OF PETER'S NISSAN 4-WHEEL-DRIVE
NAUGHTIEST DEED: BAILING-UP PEOPLE WITH HATS
PET HATE: PEOPLE WITH HATS
FAVOURITE TOY: BACK SEAT OF PETER'S NISSAN 4-WHEEL-DRIVE
KNOWN ACCOMPLICE: MAX

**PETER LEHMANN WINES** TANUNDA, SA | ALSATIAN, 10 | OWNER: PETER LEHMANN

PET HATE: PHOTOGRAPHERS
FAVOURITE TOY: LASER POINTER
KNOWN ACCOMPLICE: BILL THE GOAT
OBSESSION: BURROWING UNDER BLANKETS
FAVOURITE PASTIME: BARKING AT THE POSSUMS
NAUGHTIEST DEED: JUMPING ONTO THE BED AFTER SWIMMING IN THE DAM

OWNERS: JOHN AND ANITA WETTENHALL | JACK RUSSELL TERRIER, 5 | EAST ARM VINEYARD, HILLWOOD, TAS

45

OBSESSION: FOOD
NAUGHTIEST DEED: BITING COCO'S TEATS
PET HATE: FOUR-TEN
FAVOURITE TOY: FOUR-TEN'S TAIL

ALGY

OBSESSION: FOOD
PET HATE: BEDTIME
FAVOURITE TOY: FOUR-TEN'S TAIL
KNOWN ACCOMPLICE: SCRAMBLE
NAUGHTIEST DEED: CHEWING SHOE LACES

**GOONA WARRA** SUNBURY, VIC | SMOOTH FOX TERRIERS, 9 WEEKS | OWNER: NICK BICKFORD

OBSESSION: FOOD
NAUGHTIEST DEED: BITING COCO'S TEATS
FASTEST MEAL CONSUMED: MOTHER'S MILK
PET HATE: HAVING TAIL BITTEN
FAVOURITE TOY: PILLOW

OBSESSION: RABBITS
PET HATE: HUMAN BREATH
FAVOURITE TOY: SOCCER BALL
KNOWN ACCOMPLICE: BAXTER
FAVOURITE PASTIME: VERMIN HUNTING

COCO

OWNER: NICK BICKFORD | SMOOTH FOX TERRIERS, 9 WEEKS AND 3 YEARS | **GOONA WARRA** SUNBURY, VIC | 47

**GROWLER**

OBSESSIONS: CATS AND RABBITS
PET HATE: BEING PHOTOGRAPHED
FAVOURITE BOOK: THE CAT IN THE HAT
FASTEST MEAL CONSUMED: PAN-FRIED PORK WITH HONEY GLAZE
FAVOURITE PASTIME: TREMBLING OUTSIDE THE WINDOW IN VIEW OF DINING PUNTERS

KNOWN ACCOMPLICE: BERT
OBSESSION: LICKING PEOPLE
PET HATE: BEING SHAMPOOED
FAVOURITE TOY: PLASTIC BOTTLES
FAVOURITE PASTIMES: CHASING CATS AND RABBITS
NAUGHTIEST DEED: EATING $4000 WORTH OF TUNNEL HOUSE WALL
FASTEST MEAL CONSUMED: PRUNER'S LUNCH, STILL IN THE WRAPPING

WALDO

*" I think if I weren't so beautiful,*
*maybe I'd have more character. "*

——— **JERRY HALL**

# THE CORK TAINT
## DETECTION HOUND
*by Max Allen*

## As every wine lover knows,

*the more you drink, the more fact begins to resemble*

*fiction. Or the other way around. Or both.*

*A couple of years ago, a wonderfully funny little satirical*
*publication appeared called* Oberon Kant's Big Book of Wine *(you can still find the odd*
*copy lurking on some bookshop shelves if you're lucky), with the fictional Kant taking*
*the role of a vinous Sir Les Patterson, cocking his leg at the pomp and pretentiousness*
*of the wine world.*

*In the chapter on tasting, Kant recommends every wine neophyte arm himself or*
*herself with some essential equipment – glasses, corkscrews, decanters and a dog.*

*"In these days of ever-increasing accusations that wines can be tainted by the corks*
*that seal them," Kant writes, "I find more and more professional tasters and amateurs*
*are employing the services of a tasting hound. The hound – preferably a short-haired*
*Airedale – is sent into the room where the tasting is to take place and will sniff each*
*bottle, savaging any sommelier who dares to serve less-than-perfect wine."*

*The other day, I was quietly going about my business as a diligent and fearless wine*
*critic – which means finding a patch of clear tabletop among the mountains of press*
*releases on which to perch a couple of glasses and a bottle or two. As usual, Charlie*
*the chocolate labrador was curled up beside me (ever since I read a profile of the*
*world's most famous wine critic, Robert Parker, describing his office as a place*

*"where the family's bulldog and basset hound like to lie on the tile floor and sleep and fart and snore" I've made sure my dogs are always around when I taste).*

*The serene mood was quickly shattered, though, when I pulled the cork from a bottle. Suddenly, Charlie scrambled to his feet, as though he'd heard a possum on the roof, looked straight at the cork, took one sniff and then bolted out the door.*

*I tentatively held the cork to my nose and was assaulted by the unmistakable invisible cloud of our old enemy, 2-4-6 trichloroanisole: cork taint.*

*Crikey. Perhaps it's not such a joke after all. Just think of the possibilities. With a bit of training, some clever marketing and a nice juicy development grant from the government, this idea might have legs.*

*Wine lovers could take their cork taint detection hounds with them wherever they went. Uppity wine-waiters in posh restaurants would be quickly put back in their box by a growl from your sniffing-nose dog. Bottle shops would be far more obliging about replacing tainted bottles when confronted by an aggressive tasting terrier. And it would save an enormous amount of time at big wine exhibitions: you could just send the wine man's best friend off to sniff out and retrieve the best bottles.*

*Oberon was obviously onto something, the silly old bugger. Or he would have been, if he was real.*

MAX ALLEN IS WINE COLUMNIST FOR THE *WEEKEND AUSTRALIAN MAGAZINE* AND *GOURMET TRAVELLER*, AND PRESENTS A WINE SEGMENT ON CHANNEL 7's *BETTER HOMES AND GARDENS*. HIS LATEST PUBLICATION IS *THE REALLY USEFUL POCKET WINE BOOK* (HARDIE GRANT BOOKS). HE HAS TWO BOISTEROUS CHOCOLATE LABRADORS, CHARLIE (4) AND COCO (2), AND NOT MUCH LAWN.

**COCO**

OBSESSION: LICKING
PET HATE: POSSUM
FAVOURITE TOY: POSSUM
FASTEST MEAL CONSUMED: POSSUM
FAVOURITE PASTIME: CHEWING CHARLIE'S EARS
NAUGHTIEST DEED: STEALING A WHOLE PAVLOVA OFF THE DINING TABLE
... AND A CHRISTMAS PUDDING ... AND A CHOCOLATE CAKE

**CHARLIE**

NAUGHTIEST DEED: STEALING A
WHOLE QUICHE OFF THE DINING TABLE
PET HATE: SUSPICIOUS-LOOKING STRANGERS
WEARING SUNGLASSES DELIVERING WINE
FAVOURITE PASTIME: WAITING FOR SUSPICIOUS-
LOOKING STRANGERS WEARING
SUNGLASSES DELIVERING WINE
FASTEST MEAL CONSUMED: A FOOTBALL SOCK

OWNER: MAX ALLEN | LABRADORS, 2 AND 4 | **OBERON KANT ESTATE** VIC    53

PET HATE: SOMEONE WE CAN'T NAME
FAVOURITE TOY: HER BED
KNOWN ACCOMPLICES: CLIVE AND MAX
FAVOURITE PASTIME: TOLERATING THE HENS
OBSESSION: IN HER PRIME, WORKING SHEEP AND CATTLE

JESS

OBSESSION: HIDING BEHIND BUSHES
NAUGHTIEST DEED: EATING WOODEN SPOONS
PET HATE: THE VACUUM CLEANER
FAVOURITE PASTIMES: RUNNING, EATING AND SLEEPING IN THE SUN

POPPY

OBSESSION: REAR ENDS OF ALL SPECIES

NAUGHTIEST DEED: EATING JANCIS ROBINSON'S
WINE COURSE VIDEOS

FAVOURITE TOY: PINE CONES

KNOWN ACCOMPLICES: CHESTER, ANGUS
AND MILLY THE DEAF CAT

FASTEST MEAL CONSUMED: THE CAT'S FOOD EVERY MORNING

PET HATE: DISCIPLINE

OBSESSIONS: UNDERWEAR AND STARING AT THE CHOOKS

NAUGHTIEST DEEDS: EATING THE VINEYARD OWNER'S FAVOURITE
STRAW HAT WHILST STANDING ON THEIR DINING ROOM TABLE

FAVOURITE PASTIMES: PEEING ON THINGS
AND QUALITY CONTROL AT VINTAGE

MANTONS CREEK VINEYARD MAIN RIDGE, VIC | BRITTANY SPANIELS, 1 | OWNERS: ALEX AND GINNY EDGAR

MERLOT

FAVOURITE PASTIME: CHASING MICE AND RABBITS
KNOWN ACCOMPLICES: ZELL, MAJOR, REX AND CINDY
OBSESSIONS: GREETING CUSTOMERS, MORNING WALKS AND PLAYING WITH CHILDREN

OBSESSION: *LEANING ON FAMILY MEMBERS*
NAUGHTIEST DEED: *SNEAKING BONES INSIDE*
FAVOURITE TOY: *PLAYING WITH FAMILY MEMBERS' FEET*
FAVOURITE PASTIME: *SEARCHING FOR FOOD*
KNOWN ACCOMPLICE: *MARGARET (PICTURED)*

PET HATE: *ALL LOUD NOISES*
FAVOURITE TOY: *TOY ECHIDNA*
FAVOURITE PASTIME: *HIDING UNDER THE BED*
NAUGHTIEST DEED: *CLIMBING TREES TO ESCAPE*
OBSESSION: *RUBBING HER BEARD ALONG THE RUG*
FASTEST MEAL CONSUMED: *BELGIUM CHOCOLATE*
KNOWN ACCOMPLICE: *LINDSAY (PICTURED)*

KNOWN ACCOMPLICE: TOSCA
PET HATE: FOXES IN VINEYARD AT NIGHT
OBSESSION: CHEESE AND BISCUITS AT THE CELLAR DOOR
NAUGHTIEST DEED: DUCKLING HUNTING ON THE DAM
FAVOURITE TOY: HEADLESS ELEPHANT SOFT TOY
FASTEST MEAL CONSUMED: FOOD FROM SMALL CHILDREN
FAVOURITE PASTIME: ROAMING THE VINEYARD WITH TOSCA

SIENA

OBSESSION: LOOKING FOR RABBITS
NAUGHTIEST DEED: INTIMIDATING NEIGHBOURHOOD SHEEP
PET HATES: HOME DETENTION AND VETS
FAVOURITE TOY: STUFFED SHAR PEI
KNOWN ACCOMPLICES: POLLY AND CLOVIS
FAVOURITE PASTIMES: SLEEPING AND DRESSING IN HUMAN CLOTHES
FAVOURITE TV CHANNEL: ANIMAL PLANET

| **NO. 1 FAMILY ESTATE** BLENHEIM, NZ | SHAR PEI, 9 | OWNER: REMY LE BRUN

PET HATE: THE GEESE
FAVOURITE TOY: THE GEESE
NAUGHTIEST DEED: CHASING CHOOKS
FASTEST MEAL CONSUMED: A WORKER'S LUNCH
KNOWN ACCOMPLICES: JACKSON AND ELIZA MATTHEWS
FAVOURITE PASTIME: CHASING GIRL DOGS
FAVOURITE MOVIE: A FISH CALLED WANDA

SCOTT

JEDDA

OBSESSION: FETCHING BALLS.
FAVOURITE TOY: ROPE TOY
KNOWN ACCOMPLICE: CHAIM
FAVOURITE PASTIMES: SURFING AND SWIMMING
NAUGHTIEST DEED: CHEWING SHOES AND SANDALS

| **HAPPS** DUNSBOROUGH, WA | FLAT-COATED RETRIEVER, 2 | OWNERS: ROSLYN AND ERL HAPP

KNOWN ACCOMPLICE: FRANK
PET HATES: CATS AND WAVES
OBSESSIONS: FOOTBALLS AND MUM
FAVOURITE TOYS: MILK CARTONS AND PLASTIC BOTTLES
NAUGHTIEST DEED: SETTING HIMSELF IN QUICKSET CONCRETE
FASTEST MEAL CONSUMED: MOTHER-IN-LAW'S LAMB FRENCH CUTLETS

OWNERS: PAUL AND KATE BOULDEN | BORDER COLLIE, 4 | **SANDALFORD WINES** CAVERSHAM, WA

PET HATE: FULL SAIL WHEN ON THE YACHT
FAVOURITE TOYS: RODERICK, MARY, MARGOT
KNOWN ACCOMPLICES: SADIE AND REG
OBSESSION: HAVING HER OWN CHAIR ON THE VERANDAH
FAVOURITE PASTIME: VIGILANTE NIGHT TRIPS TO WARN OFF INTRUDERS

FLEK

OBSESSION: BALLS
NAUGHTIEST DEED: PUTTING BALL BETWEEN PEOPLE'S LEGS
FAVOURITE TOY: BALLS
FASTEST MEAL CONSUMED: CHICKEN NECKS
KNOWN ACCOMPLICE: RUBY RED
FAVOURITE PASTIME: CATCHING THE BALL BEFORE IT BOUNCES

TRUE BLUE

**BEAR**

OBSESSION: DIGGING HOLES
NAUGHTIEST DEED: EATING THE NEW LOUNGE SUITE
PET HATE: VACUUM CLEANER
KNOWN ACCOMPLICE: JEDDA
FAVOURITE PASTIME: SLEEPING

PET HATE: TEA TOWELS
FAVOURITE TOY: BEAR
OBSESSION: GOING FOR A WALK
NAUGHTIEST DEED: CHEWING LEGS OFF KITCHEN TABLE

**JEDDA**

**LEEUWIN ESTATE** MARGARET RIVER, WA | ROTTWEILER, 3 AND JACK RUSSELL, 5 | OWNERS: BOYD AND GATI WRIGHT

PET HATE: BATHTIME
OBSESSION: SNORKELLING
NAUGHTIEST DEED: NICKING SAUSAGES OFF THE BBQ
FAVOURITE TOY: STONES IN THE VINEYARD
FASTEST MEAL CONSUMED: JOINT OF FINEST BEEF
KNOWN ACCOMPLICES: ALICE THE AIREDALE AND SCOTTIE McTAVISH
FAVOURITE PASTIME: CHASING STONES
FAVOURITE TV SHOW: TOM AND JERRY

PIPPIN

**PATCH**

PET HATE: THE BOSS'S BOOT
OBSESSION: CHASING CARS
NAUGHTIEST DEED: DOING BOMBS IN THE OFFICE
FASTEST MEAL CONSUMED: ALL FOOD ESPECIALLY CHOCOLATE
KNOWN ACCOMPLICE: MAVERICK THE CAT
FAVOURITE PASTIME: SLEEPING ON HIS BEANBAG

FORREST ESTATE WINERY RENWICK NZ | WIRE-HAIRED TERRIER 12 | OWNERS: BRIGID AND JOHN FORREST

PET HATE: PLASTIC BAGS
OBSESSION: NOISY BIRDS
KNOWN ACCOMPLICE: THE CAT
FAVOURITE TOYS: BALLS AND BUNGS FROM BARRELS
FASTEST MEAL CONSUMED: ANYTHING EXCEPT LETTUCE
FAVOURITE PLACE: SLEEPING IN HER BARREL
FAVOURITE PASTIME: CHASING RABBITS THEN RUNNING PAST THEM

OWNER: GARY FARR (PICTURED) | KELPIE, 4 | BY FARR BANNOCKBURN, VIC

**SHADOW**

OBSESSION: CHASING VIBRATIONS
PET HATES: CATS AND CARS
KNOWN ACCOMPLICES:
VINEYARD WORKERS AND
HELEN AND JIM'S GRANDCHILDREN

| **FOX CREEK WINES** WILLUNGA, SA | BORDER COLLIE, 5 | OWNERS: HELEN AND JIM WATTS

shadow *has been part of the Fox Creek Winery family ever since Helen Watts saved him from certain doom as she waited with her cat at the local veterinary. Helen has a sharp eye for a smart dog and left the vet that day with a new best friend. The cat has never forgiven her.*

*Shadow is an eccentric border collie who spends his entire time helping around the vineyard and cellar door. When the pruner's secateurs hit the trellis wire, the wire vibrates and Shadow chases the vibration up and down the vineyard rows. This can go on for several hours or even all day. Shadow loves it and so do we!*

OBSESSION: THE COUCH
PET HATE: DOMESTIC SPARKLING
NAUGHTIEST DEED: SNEAKING OUT FOR A CRYSTAL
FAVOURITE PASTIME: WATCHING TV FROM THE COUCH

KNOWN ACCOMPLICE: MILLI
FAVOURITE TOY: CHAMPAGNE CORKS
FASTEST MEAL CONSUMED: CONFIT AND FOIS GRAS
FAVOURITE PASTIME: WATCHING TV FROM THE COUCH

PERI AND MOGWAI

OBSESSION: KEEPING UP
WITH PERI AND MOGWAI
FASTEST MEAL CONSUMED: A SHOE
KNOWN ACCOMPLICES: PERI AND MOGWAI

OBSESSION: SPORT SHOES
FAVOURITE FILM: GREMLINS
FAVOURITE PASTIME: POLISHING FLOORBOARDS
FASTEST MEAL CONSUMED: ANOTHER SHOE
KNOWN ACCOMPLICES: BOLLI, RUDI AND HENRI

ELLY

KNOWN ACCOMPLICE: MOLLY
PET HATE: THE SUN IN HER EYES
NAUGHTIEST DEED: CHEWING ALL THE OFFICE COMPUTER CABLES
FAVOURITE PASTIME: RUNNING UP VINEYARD HILL AT 40 KM/H
OBSESSIONS: PIGEONS, OTHER PEOPLE'S FOOD AND PRUNER'S LUNCH BOXES

**great mystery solved!** *The key to one of the wine world's oldest mysteries has finally been solved. It is estimated that every winemaker, pruner or vineyard worker mysteriously loses their lunch at least twice during a season. On average, that's over 25,000 lunches that disappear annually in the Australasian wine industry alone.*

*This could easily be explained in areas such as the Margaret River, due to their abnormally high reports of UFO sightings. And of course Marlborough has their legendary winemaker that steals other workers' lunches when they're not looking. But still, it doesn't explain the other 22,000 lunches that go missing ... until now.*

*The key to the mystery lies in the hundreds of innocent faces within these pages. With the flash of the camera in their eyes and the promise of more Schmackos if they cooperated – dogs rolled over faster than a rabbit at a Dapto greyhounds meet ... and the mystery was solved – Gulp!*

**BELLA**

OBSESSION: FOOD
PET HATE: GETTING WET
KNOWN ACCOMPLICE: SPYDA
FAVOURITE TOY: ANYTHING THAT SHE IS NOT SUPPOSED TO HAVE
FAVOURITE PASTIME: GREETING CUSTOMERS IN CELLAR DOOR

**CHARLES MELTON WINES** TANUNDA, SA │ DALMATIAN, 4 │ OWNERS: CHARLIE AND VIRGINIA MELTON

OBSESSION: SNAKES
PET HATES: LOUD NOISES AND THUNDER
FAVOURITE TOY: HIS OLD JUMPER
KNOWN ACCOMPLICE: HARRY
FAVOURITE PASTIME: GOING FOR A WALK

GUS

ALBERT

FASTEST MEAL CONSUMED: PIZZA
OBSESSIONS: CHEWING PILLOWS AND DOING PILATES
NAUGHTIEST DEED: EATING KELLY'S FAVOURITE DRESS
PET HATE: HEAVY METAL MUSIC AND BEING CALLED A LABRADOODLE
FAVOURITE PASTIME: CHASING COWS AND NATIVE HENS

**HOME HILL WINES** RANELAGH, TAS | CURLY-COATED RETRIEVER, 1 | OWNER: KELLY BENNETT

BEST FRIEND: JEN
OBSESSIONS: WATER AND CAR KEYS
PET HATES: HAIRDRYERS AND FERRETS
FASTEST MEAL CONSUMED: SCHMACKOS
FAVOURITE PASTIME: DE-RABBITING THE VINEYARD
NAUGHTIEST DEED: CHASING WEDGE-TAILED EAGLES OUT OF THE GARDEN
SPECIAL TALENT: CLIMBING UP AND HIDING HIS BONE IN THE MULBERRY TREE

MOG

DAISY

OBSESSION: DESTRUCTION
NAUGHTIEST DEED: EATING THREE OF HER OWN BEDS
FAVOURITE TOY: ANYTHING THAT CAN BE CHEWED
FASTEST MEAL CONSUMED: ANYTHING CONTAINING CHICKEN
KNOWN ACCOMPLICES: COCO AND NELLIE

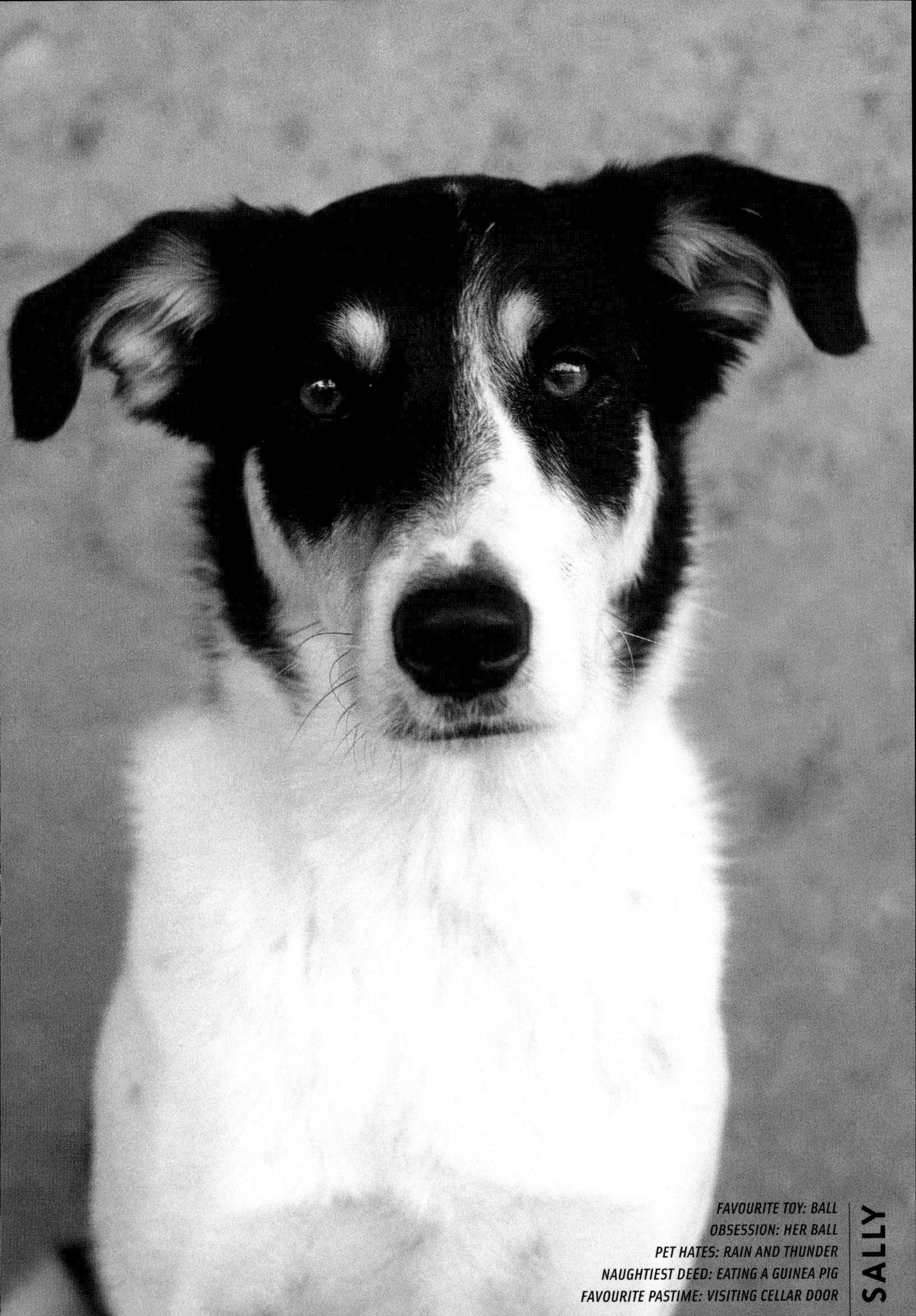

FAVOURITE TOY: BALL
OBSESSION: HER BALL
PET HATES: RAIN AND THUNDER
NAUGHTIEST DEED: EATING A GUINEA PIG
FAVOURITE PASTIME: VISITING CELLAR DOOR

SALLY

OWNER: PETER AND LINDA JENKINS | BORDER COLLIE / KELPIE X, 2 | **ISLAND BROOK ESTATE** METRICUP, WA

**MERLE**

FAVOURITE TOY: BANKSIA FLOWERS
KNOWN ACCOMPLICE: INDIANA NOON.
OBSESSION: CHASING VINEYARD RABBITS
NAUGHTIEST DEED: KILLING OUR LAST EGG-LAYING CHOOK
PET HATE: THE CAT GETTING TOO MUCH ATTENTION
FAVOURITE PASTIME: MONITORING MEAL TIMES OF FAMILY MEMBERS

**NOON WINERY** McLAREN VALE, SA | GREAT DANE, 11 MONTHS | OWNERS: DREW AND RAEGAN NOON

OSCAR

PET HATE: BATH TIME
OBSESSION: CHASING SHEEP AND GOATS
NAUGHTIEST DEED: STILL LEARNING TO BE NAUGHTY

FAVOURITE PASTIME:
TORMENTING THE CAT, FLUFFY
FASTEST MEAL CONSUMED: MINCED MEAT
FAVOURITE TOY: BALL ON A ROPE

OSCAR

*PET HATE: WATER*
*FAVOURITE TOY: AN OLD LAMB SHANK*
*NAUGHTIEST DEED: PEEING IN THE RAIN GAUGE*
*FASTEST MEAL CONSUMED: THE NEXT ONE*

TWIGGY

PET HATE: CYCLISTS
OBSESSION: PALLET TROLLEY
FAVOURITE TOY: ANY PLASTIC BOTTLE
NAUGHTIEST DEED: STEALING PICKERS' LUNCHES
FASTEST MEAL CONSUMED: PÂTÉ LEFT OVER FROM PLATTERS
FAVOURITE PASTIME: CHASING ANYTHING THAT MOVES (EXCEPT PEOPLE)

OWNER: PAULA KLOOSTERMAN | HEELER/WHIPPET X, 2 | FREYCINET VINEYARDS BICHENO, TAS

OBSESSION: PURE WOOL SOCKS
PET HATE: GARBAGE TRUCK
FASTEST MEAL CONSUMED: A CARAMELISED
PEAR OFF A GUEST'S PLATE
FAVOURITE PASTIME: SLEEPING ON
THE BED IF THE DOOR GETS LEFT OPEN

OBSESSION: BARKING AT POSSUMS
PET HATE: COMING INSIDE WHEN SHE'S ONTO A POSSUM
FAVOURITE TOY: ANYTHING SMALL AND LIVE
FASTEST MEAL CONSUMED: ANYTHING PEDRO MIGHT WANT
FAVOURITE PASTIME: PULLING PEDRO'S TAIL
WHEN HE'S TRYING TO SLEEP

**ANADA**

| **PENFOLDS** NURIOOTPA, SA | GOLDEN RETRIEVERS, 4 AND 2 | OWNERS: NICK GILL AND ANGELA CLIFFORD

KNOWN ACCOMPLICE: MUSTY
PET HATES: RUNNERS AND JOGGERS
NAUGHTIEST DEED: SLEEPING ON THE COUCH
FAVOURITE PASTIME: SLEEPING NEXT TO THE FIRE
FAVOURITE TOYS: DOVES AND ANY FEATHERED SPECIES
OBSESSION: RETRIEVING STICKS BUT NEVER RETURNING THEM

**MAX**

BLUEY

OBSESSION: CATS
NAUGHTIEST DEED: EATING CAR SEAT BELTS
PET HATES: SOME OF OUR FRIENDS
FAVOURITE TOYS: TENNIS BALL OR PINE CONES
KNOWN ACCOMPLICE: BILLY

**ELGEE PARK WINES** MERRICKS NTH, VIC | BLUE HEELER, 10 | OWNERS: SARAH AND BAILS MYER

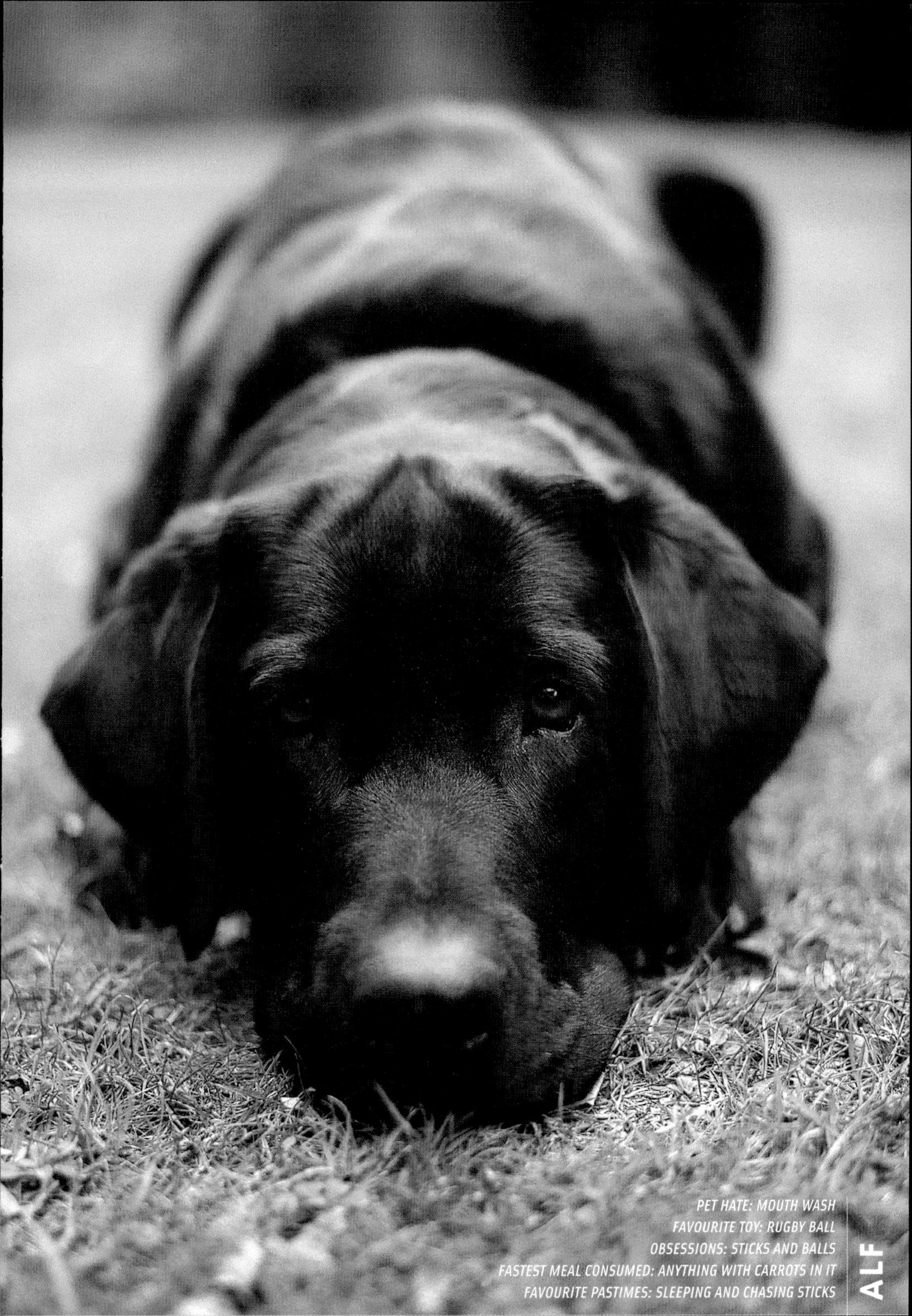

PET HATE: MOUTH WASH
FAVOURITE TOY: RUGBY BALL
OBSESSIONS: STICKS AND BALLS
FASTEST MEAL CONSUMED: ANYTHING WITH CARROTS IN IT
FAVOURITE PASTIMES: SLEEPING AND CHASING STICKS

ALF

OWNER: CP LIN | LABRADOR, 5 | **MOUNTFORD VINEYARD** WAIPARA, NZ

*" From the dog's point of view,*
*his master is an elongated*
*and abnormally cunning dog."*

——— MABEL LOUISE ROBINSON

OBSESSION: VANDALISM
PET HATE: BEING LOCKED UP
NAUGHTIEST DEED: ATE PRESCRIPTION GLASSES AND MOBILE PHONE
FAVOURITE TOYS: TOILET ROLLS, FRISBEE AND SQUEAKY BALL
FASTEST MEAL CONSUMED: FOUR BLUE-EYE COD FILLETS
KNOWN ACCOMPLICES: DAISY AND NELLIE

COCO

OWNER: GREG AND JULES JARRATT | LABRADOR, 1 | **COLDSTREAM HILLS** COLDSTREAM, VIC | 93

ISABELLE

PET HATE: WATER
OBSESSION: MICHAEL'S SLIPPERS
NAUGHTIEST DEED: EATING THE BED
FAVOURITE TOY: A TOY CHICKEN
KNOWN ACCOMPLICE: SASSOON
FAVOURITE PASTIME: PLAY FIGHTING SASSOON

**MOORILLA ESTATE** BERRIEDALE, TAS | LABRADOR, 6 MONTHS | OWNER: MICHAEL GLOVER

OBSESSIONS: FOOD AND WATER
PET HATE: WINE WRITERS
KNOWN ACCOMPLICE: MICHAEL
FAVOURITE PASTIME: SWIMMING
NAUGHTIEST DEED: EATING FOOD FROM THE KITCHEN BENCH

SASSOON

PET HATES: BATHS AND RAIN
FAVOURITE TOY: PLASTIC CONTAINERS
OBSESSIONS: CHASING GO-KARTS AND THE OCCASIONAL CAT
NAUGHTIEST DEED: EATING THE PET SILKY BANTAM CHICKENS
FASTEST MEAL CONSUMED: KANGAROO MINCE AND NOODLES
KNOWN ACCOMPLICE: ANDREAS HENSCHKE
FAVOURITE PASTIME: SINGING TO THE SOUND OF A SAXOPHONE

**HENSCHKE** KEYNETON, SA | SMOOTH-HAIRED DACHSHUND, 9 | OWNERS: PRUE AND STEPHEN HENSCHKE

FAVOURITE TOY: RABBITS
PET HATE: EARS BEING TUGGED
OBSESSIONS: CHASING CHICKENS AND RABBITS
FAVOURITE PASTIME: CHASING RABBITS
NAUGHTIEST DEED: PUTTING HIS NOSE WHERE IT SHOULDN'T BE

ALBY

*"All knowledge, the totality*
*of all questions and all answers,*
*is contained in the dog."*

——————— **FRANZ KAFKA**

# IT'S A DOG'S DINNER

*by Chester Osborn*

**the year is 3105.** *Over the past thousand years, genetic engineering had changed everything. In a desire to give humans a superior sense of smell and taste, and to improve their winemaking, a dog gene was introduced into new generations. The results backfired as the new race's heightened senses meant that they disliked wine immensely, as it all tasted too bitter and strong. However, dogs were well known to be partial to a good beverage. So it was decided to give dogs the human gene for speech. This way they could tell humans what the wine smelt and tasted like, enabling them to make superior wines.*

*The gene for intelligence was also incorporated into the dog so that they could remember the special characters of wine. These dogs would be particularly sought after. The effects changed the world dramatically. Not only did the dogs take over the winemaking, but as humans desired more recreation time and grew increasingly lazy, their dogs learnt to do everything humans could do and often did it better.*

*It wasn't long before a total role reversal occurred and dogs ruled the humans. In this new hierarchy, dogs lived in the houses and humans (now named robots – the Egyptian word for slaves) lived in sheds out the back.*

*In the new dog world, robots did most things at the dog's will, but if the dog considered the job to be fun they retained the work for themselves. Bigger dogs became the wealthiest, having the most robots to do their chores. Dogs now made all of the wine and just the way they liked it. Strangely, the vast majority of wine from a given variety and region was produced to taste all the same as all dogs had the same ideal perfect sense of taste. Ironically, robots remembered the stories back to the year 2000 when a country named Australia also made the majority of its wine taste the same. Since most of it was made from chardonnay, shiraz and cabernet sauvignon, wine in this era was somewhat boring to the masses.*

*The change started over the next few decades with the proliferation and spread of a wide array of varieties and genetic cross-breeding.*

*But in the year 3105, dogs were getting a bit lackadaisical about wine because of its uniformness. Even though there was a vast array of different varieties they did taste somewhat the same. Change was afoot. It began with a robot named Chester who would beg to make the wine. One day his master Alby dog had arranged a day at the beach, but the winery was starting to run out of wine. "Chester, you make the wine today," Alby said before leaving. Upon his return, Alby asked for a glass of tempnotaz (a genetically modified red grape incorporating tempranillos' longer tannins, pinot noir's great flowery fruit and shiraz's rich gutsy structure).*

*The wine was made with a recent invention of oak tubes, which made barrels obsolete. Tubes were immersed in the wine and air pumped through, making use of all four sides of the wood instead of one side as with barrels. This made a more efficient use of the oak. Also the vapour out-stream (alcohol and volatile wine and oak constituents) were collected and returned to the wine.*

*Alby was beautifully humoured by Chester's attempt at making tempnotaz and said, "From now on you make the wine, however under no circumstances are you allowed to swallow any." It was perfectly fine for dogs to dwell around drunk. In fact, dogs that can consume large amounts of wine and spin endless humorous yarns are the envy of all other dogs. Robots were killed on the spot if found a little drunk. They were also never allowed to laugh or tell jokes. Laughing by robots was likened to barking by the pre-genetically modified dogs, quite an obnoxious effect. If a robot was found laughing, a laugh inhibitor was attached to the neck to prevent the reoccurrence. This is quite an uncomfortable device, making neck movements almost impossible.*

*So over the years all robots forgot how to laugh and nobody missed it. Their entire existence was to be obedient to the dogs and to maintain composure at all times.*

*Gradually over the years it became very fashionable to have robots make the wines. It became quite a talking point of dogs. As he grew older, Chester's position was to make the wines and also to be Alby dog's butler. This involved going to many wine tastings to purchase the latest and greatest new robot wine. This was the new booming category of wines – one of Chester's wines sold recently for $12 million (about the same price as a new Volkswagen).*

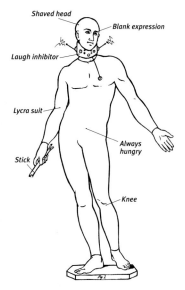

*Alby was quite proud of his robot's wines and the income it was generating. One day Alby decided to throw a dinner party inviting his most humorous wine-loving dog friends. Chester's job was to think about who was coming to dinner and to decide the appropriate order in which to drink each wine. During past dinners, Chester would stand in the corner of the dining room and watch all of the dogs as they consumed each wine, listening to every comment to build up an understanding of which wines were most appreciated. He also learnt what was appropriate, given the stature of the dogs and their preferred style.*

*Everybody turned up in fancy dress. That is, the dogs were dressed up – not the robots, as it was law that all robots wear a tight, grey, full body, one-piece Lycra-like neutral outfit. Robots had all their hair removed, as it was considered a very dirty thing to find human hair around, even though stray dog hair was prolific. Alby came dressed as a horse named Footbolt – a racehorse that his ancestors owned over a century ago.*

*The food part of the dinner was a gourmet extravaganza which was beyond description, but the interesting focus was on the wines.*

*The first wine of the evening was Chester's 'The Token Cheapskate'. This wine was made from a rare old variety called sauvignon blanc. All of the wines for this dinner were made from very old varieties except for the evening's last wine. It was fashionable for wines to be named after what the dogs particularly liked doing.*

*The next wine was to be brought from a winery named 'Not Board', owned by the dogs Jessie and Sally. Their robot winemaker Robert O'Callaghan was also present. Unfortunately they had left the wines in the basket on their kitchen table. The next wine came from a neighbour dog named Bella who came dressed in an ancient history costume worn by humans, namely moleskin pants and a blue shirt and pull-on boots. Bella was accompanied by robot winemaker Charlie Melton. Their wine was quite popular, named 'Find Hopes' made from a variety that once was the number one variety in the world. However, grenache is nearly extinct now.*

*The third wine was from dogs Dirk and Booph. Both came dressed as robot hunters. It was a red wine called 'Shave Hard', something that dogs hoped robots would do. Their robot winemaker Iain Riggs was also present. Wines four, five and six all came from a dog dressed in an ancient comical costume called lederhosen. Her name was Cassie. They were all reds made in an old-fashioned way from varieties that only existed in these vineyards and were considered interesting but not worth carrying on about. The wines were named 'Count Medals Son', 'See the Hens' Teeth' and 'Mill the Waste'. The proud robot winemaker Stephen Henschke was also present.*

*Number seven was brought by dogs Solomon and Fronti, who had forgotten to dress up. An interesting wine from unknown varieties. The wine named 'Are you welding'. Robot winemaker Tim Adams came along for the ride.*

Dog Bronson brought wine eight. He came in the nude but with a massive wig covering all. The wine was named 'Phone Hell' after the warm holiday venue near the equator located under Russia. It was believed the wine was made from at least 20 varieties as this winery knew all the tricks. Robot winemaker Peter Lehmann was present.

A neighbouring dog named Teal dressed in torn clothes brought wine number nine called 'Fun Dig'. Robot winemaker David Powell joined his master.

Alby provided wine ten, 'The Farting Bagpipe', made mainly from a red grape Zarihs co-fermented with three obscure white grapes and wine number eleven, named 'The Wed Yarn'. This was a straight Zarihs highly sought after. The name referred to a great yarn about an ancient humorous habit of monogamy called wedded. The last wine was brought by Dog Toby who dressed up as a river (quite a smelly, not that wet, salty river). The wine was called 'The Nobel 23', a sparkling very sweet red made from Gamanet grapes (a cross from two very old grape varieties rarely used called gamey and cabernet). The grapes were left on the vine a long time to get infected with lots of different rots. The robot winemaker Darren De Bortoli was also present.

When the dinner was nearly over, it was time for the annual robot-barking contest. Each robot would take their turn barking. This was a trait lost by dogs when they gained speech. The winner was robot David Powell. His bark was so loud it even woke the neighbours, a rare but highly sought-after trait.

A great time was had by all. But it was now time to go home and leave Chester with all the mess to tidy up.

CHESTER OSBORN IS CHIEF WINEMAKER AND VITICULTURIST AT D'ARENBERG, McLAREN VALE, SA.

OBSESSION: FOOD
NAUGHTIEST DEED: CATCHING A KANGAROO
PET HATE: BATHTIME
FAVOURITE TOY: FOOD
KNOWN ACCOMPLICES: JANICE AND RAHNEE
FAVOURITE PASTIMES: SLEEPING AND EATING THEN SLEEPING

**DEVIL'S LAIR** MARGARET RIVER, WA | IRISH WOLFHOUND, 5 | OWNER: STUART PYM

PET HATE: BIRDS
FAVOURITE TOY: TENNIS BALLS
OBSESSION: LICKING UP SPILT GRAPE SKINS
NAUGHTIEST DEED: EATING A LARGE WHEEL OF BRIE
FAVOURITE PASTIME: SLEEPING IN CARS
FASTEST MEAL CONSUMED: THE VINEYARD MANAGER'S BIRTHDAY CAKE

OBSESSION: BEING NOTICED
NAUGHTIEST DEED: HERDING A MOB OF COWS
PET HATE: BEING LEFT ALONE
FAVOURITE TOY: A BIG PINK TEDDY BEAR
FASTEST MEAL CONSUMED: CHINESE BARBECUED DUCK
KNOWN ACCOMPLICE: HUBERT
FAVOURITE PASTIME: BEING CUDDLED

SCHATZI

WALLACE

OBSESSION: PLAYING SOCCER
NAUGHTIEST DEED: SWALLOWING STOCKINGS, HAIRBRUSH,
SPOTLIGHT AND FOOD BOWL – ALL REQUIRING X-RAYS
PET HATE: NEXT DOOR'S MALAMUTES
FAVOURITE TOY: PANDA BEAR
FAVOURITE PASTIME: HAVING HIS STOMACH RUBBED

OBSESSION: CHASING PEOPLE'S FEET
NAUGHTIEST DEED: FAILING DOG SCHOOL
PET HATE: BEING PATTED ON THE HEAD
FAVOURITE TOY: BLANKETS TO HIDE UNDER
FAVOURITE PASTIME: SLEEPING ON PILLOWS

REGGIE

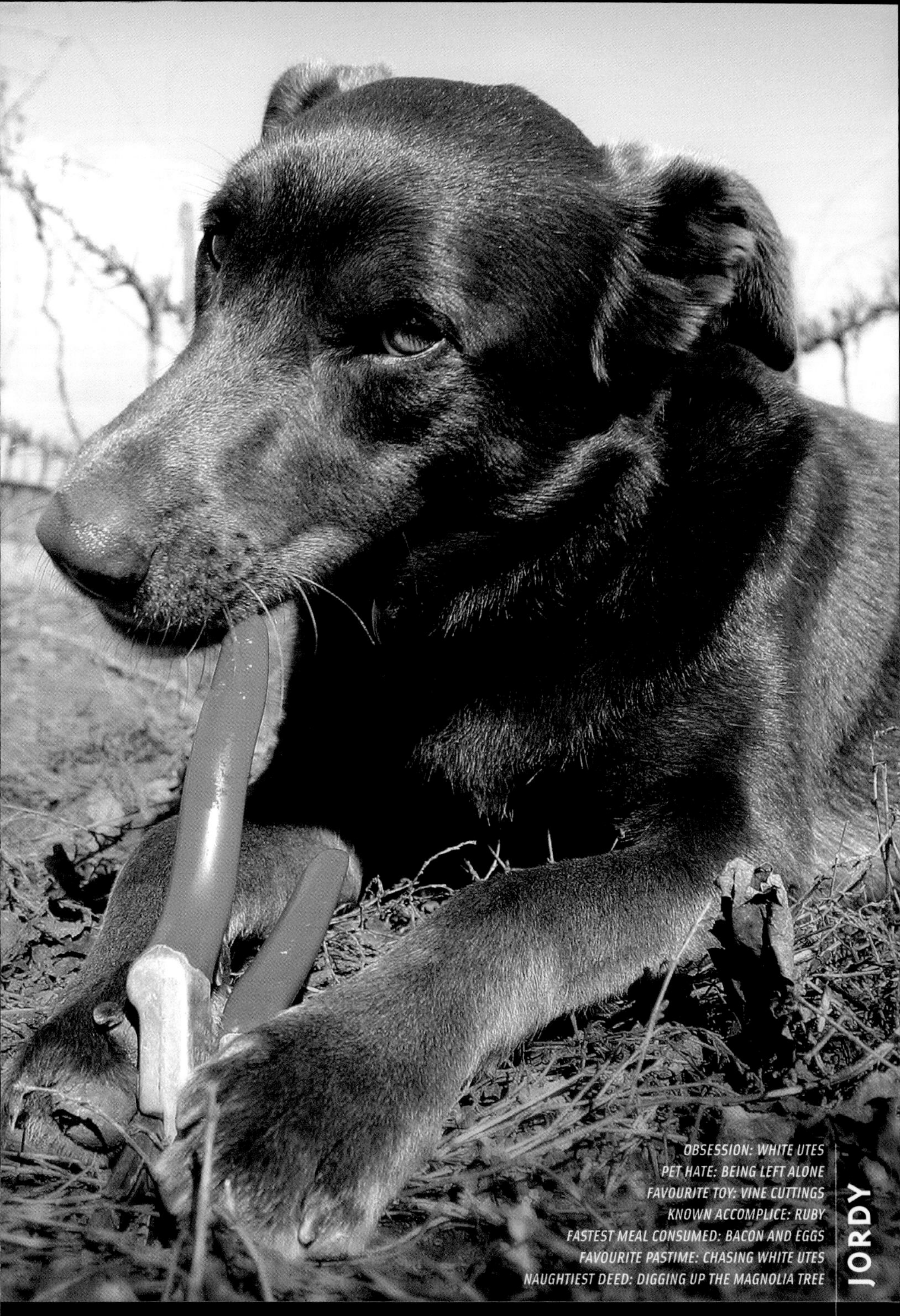

# JORDY

OBSESSION: WHITE UTES
PET HATE: BEING LEFT ALONE
FAVOURITE TOY: VINE CUTTINGS
KNOWN ACCOMPLICE: RUBY
FASTEST MEAL CONSUMED: BACON AND EGGS
FAVOURITE PASTIME: CHASING WHITE UTES
NAUGHTIEST DEED: DIGGING UP THE MAGNOLIA TREE

OWNERS: JACQUI AND BILL STEVENS | KELPIE, 2 | **STEVENS BROOK ESTATE** ECHUCA, VIC

OBSESSION: EATING GRAPES
PET HATE: GETTING INTO CARS
KNOWN ACCOMPLICE: ALBERT
FAVOURITE TOYS: LILLY AND BEAR, THE CATS
NAUGHTIEST DEED: RUNNING AWAY WITH ALBERT
FAVOURITE PASTIME: RUNNING AWAY WITH ALBERT

MOËT

**HOME HILL WINES** RANELAGH, TAS | GOLDEN RETRIEVER, 2 | OWNERS: ROSEMARY AND TERRY BENNETT

OBSESSIONS: BUNGS, STICKS AND TOURISTS AT THE CELLAR DOOR
PET HATES: WEEKENDS AND WET WEATHER
FASTEST MEAL CONSUMED: ANYTHING AFTER A LONG DAY AT THE WINERY
FAVOURITE PASTIME: LAZING IN FRONT OF THE OPEN FIRE

**RODNEY**

OBSESSION: JIMMY
PET HATE: JIMMY GETTING MORE ATTENTION THAN HIM
FAVOURITE TOY: JIMMY'S COLLAR (WHILE STILL ON JIMMY)
FAVOURITE PASTIME: HUNTING FOR RABBITS AND MICE
NAUGHTIEST DEED: RIPPING UNDERWEAR OFF THE NEIGHBOUR'S CLOTHESLINE

PET HATE: GARY GOING AWAY
FAVOURITE TOY: SQUEAKY RUBBER DUCKY
FAVOURITE MOVIE: 101 DALMATIANS
KNOWN ACCOMPLICES: ICE THE JACK RUSSELL PUPPY
AND TIGGA THE ADVENTUROUS KITTEN
OBSESSION: CHOCOLATE-COATED ROASTED ALMONDS
NAUGHTIEST DEED: STEALING GRAPE PICKERS' LUNCHES

OWNER: GARY NEALE | DALMATIAN, 10 | **BRIGHTWATER VINEYARD** NELSON, NZ    113

OBSESSION: GETTING TO WORK ON TIME (EVEN ON DAYS OFF)
NAUGHTIEST DEED: RUNNING IN FRONT OF PUSHBIKE
PET HATES: OSCAR AND BEING DISTURBED
FAVOURITE TOY: MOST COMFORTABLE BED
KNOWN ACCOMPLICE: ERMA

OBSESSION: RACING THE VINEYARD MOTORBIKES
NAUGHTIEST DEED: STEALING A NEWBORN LAMB FROM ITS MOTHER
TO KEEP HIM COMPANY IN HIS BASKET AND TO MOTHER IT
PET HATE: SMALL YAPPY DOGS
FAVOURITE TOY: HIS STUFFED RABBIT
KNOWN ACCOMPLICE: HIS BEST FRIEND ARNOLD THE CAT

WALTER

ZIGGY

OBSESSION: LISA
NAUGHTIEST DEED: STEALING
SAUSAGES OFF THE BBQ HOTPLATE
PET HATE: LISA BEING AWAY
FASTEST MEAL CONSUMED: KRISPY KREMES AND SAUSAGES
FAVOURITE PASTIME: JOGGING AROUND THE OVAL WITH LISA

**TEMPUS TWO WINES** POKOLBIN, NSW | BORDER COLLIE, 5 | OWNER: LISA McGUIGAN

# THE BLACK AND WHITE
# EMPLOYMENT AGENCY
by Robert O'Callaghan

**when I first** started Rockford it was pretty much a one-man show. I made the wine, ran the business and stood behind the counter in the cellar door sales seven days a week. I desperately needed staff but didn't have the time to organise anyone. Fate took control in the form of my dalmatian named Ben. New neighbours had moved into a house about a kilometre up Krondorf Road and they were serious bike riders. Every day they went flashing past on their high-speed racers. One day I was in the cellar door when I heard the dog let out a terrible noise so ran out expecting to see him splattered on the road. Instead I found the dog with a dumb look on his face standing next to my new neighbour tangled up in her bike covered in bits of gravel, bitumen and lots of blood. Ben had put his head into the front wheel of the bike and apart from feeling more stupid than normal was unhurt. But Lynette was in a pretty bad way so I helped her inside and while I was apologising and helping stem the flow of blood the conversation led to her telling me she was looking for a job. When she eventually healed she started at Rockford, working in cellar door sales – that was eighteen years ago. Lynette is still with Rockford and looks after our wholesale accounts in Adelaide where she is highly regarded by everyone she has contact with. Dalmatians may not be very bright but in selecting staff Ben gave me a better result than some of the very expensive employment agencies.

ROBERT O'CALLAGHAN IS CHIEF EXECUTIVE AND WINEMAKER AT ROCKFORD WINES, TANUNDA, SA.

**JESSIE**

KNOWN ACCOMPLICE: SALLY
OBSESSION: BEING UNDER THE DOONA
PET HATE: ALL OTHER DOGS EXCEPT SALLY AND DIGGER
FAVOURITE TOY: GHANDI THE WINERY CAT
NAUGHTIEST DEED: BURROWING HOLES THROUGH THE CARPET IN THE OFFICE

OBSESSION: LICKING THE INSIDE OF GHANDI'S EARS
NAUGHTIEST DEED: REJECTING OBEDIENCE
PET HATE: THE BAGSHAW CRUSHER
KNOWN ACCOMPLICES: JESSIE AND GHANDI THE WINERY CAT
FAVOURITE PASTIME: SNEAKING OUT OF THE WINERY

**SALLY**

PEGGY

PET HATE: FIONA'S CAT
FAVOURITE TOY: JOHN'S SMELLY RIDING BOOT
KNOWN ACCOMPLICES: REX AND GREY DOG
FAVOURITE PASTIME: CHASING HARES IN THE VINEYARD
NAUGHTIEST DEED: HITCHING RIDES HOME WITH VINEYARD WORKERS

**CRAWFORD RIVER WINES** CONDAH, VIC | KELPIE, 2 | OWNERS: BELINDA (PICTURED) AND JOHN THOMSON

PET HATE: HIS PAWS BEING TICKLED
FAVOURITE TOY: SQUEAKING T-BONE STEAK
KNOWN ACCOMPLICE: DOUG BOWEN
FAVOURITE PASTIME: LOBSTER FISHING
OBSESSION: RETRIEVING THE NEWSPAPER EACH MORNING

BOLLI

OBSESSIONS: FOOD AND HER BEAN-BAG
PET HATE: HAVING THE LIGHT ON AFTER 9 PM
FAVOURITE TOYS: TWO GUINEA PIG FRIENDS, ROBERT AND HENRY
KNOWN ACCOMPLICES: ROBERT AND HENRY
FAVOURITE PASTIME: LYING IN THE SUN OR ON HER BEAN BAG

FAVOURITE TOY: BOOTH'S TANKER
NAUGHTIEST DEED: TAKING CONTROL
PET HATES: THUNDER, GOOD FOOD GOING TO WASTE
OBSESSION: THE MOST COMFORTABLE SEAT IN THE HOUSE
FASTEST MEAL CONSUMED: DRIVE-THRU HUNGRY JACK'S
KNOWN ACCOMPLICES: CHRIS HOLMES, INSPECTOR REX
FAVOURITE PASTIMES: HUNTING LIONS, RESTORING ANTIQUES

ELLE

SAM

PET HATE: CATS
OBSESSION: CHASING CATS
NAUGHTIEST DEED: EATING KATE'S CHOOKS
FASTEST MEAL CONSUMED: CHOOKS
KNOWN ACCOMPLICES: THE VINTAGE STAFF
FAVOURITE PASTIMES: EATING AND SLEEPING

**TAMAR RIDGE WINES** KAYENA, TAS | KEESHOND X, 17 | OWNER: KATE NIELSEN

PET HATE: CATS
OBSESSION: AIR-DRIED BEEF
NAUGHTIEST DEED: COUCH SURFING
KNOWN ACCOMPLICE: HER DAUGHTER GEORGIE
FAVOURITE PASTIME: HARVESTING CABERNET

**FERMOY ESTATE** WILLYABRUP, WA | AIREDALE TERRIER, 3 | OWNER: ALLISON KELLY

OBSESSIONS: EATING AND RUNNING
NAUGHTIEST DEED: SPENT TWO NIGHTS IN BRUTHEN JAILHOUSE
PET HATES: MICROWAVES AND HOSES
FAVOURITE TOY: DOG BONE
KNOWN ACCOMPLICE: OSCAR

TOM

# raining dogs and dogs

*When Voyager Estate claimed to have the most dogs at a single winery in the Southern Hemisphere, we were slightly sceptical. But seeing is believing and as we arrived at the winery, woofers were everywhere. Some were too shy to be photographed, while others were on holiday leave. The rest were happy to pose for our camera but then it was back to work.*

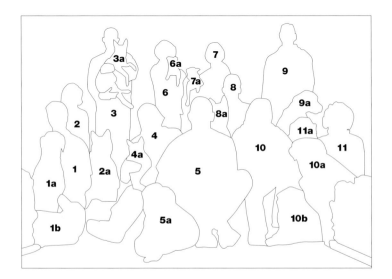

**1** *Darren Johnson*
**1a** *Brandy; Dalmatian, 3. Breaks into cars.*
**1b** *Bundy; Australian Blue Retriever, 13. Latched onto Michael Wright's trouser leg, refusing him entry into his own winery.*

**2** *Vikki Milligan-Messenger*
**2a** *Jeepers; Blue Heeler X, 4. Once stole a cricket ball mid-game.*

**3** *Kurt Schaafsma*
**3a** *Sprocket; Kelpie X, 7 months. Loves being cheeky.*

**4** *Ken Palmer*
**4a** *Spike; Fox Terrier X, 14. Hates puppies.*

**5** *Andrew Gradisen*
**5a** *Alby Woof; Australian Retriever, 8. Hates balloons and disco lights.*

**6** *Nola Leighton*
**6a** *Stella; Jack Russell Terrier, 6 months. Once ate a friend's sea dragon out of the tank.*

**7** *Jan Stocker*
**7a** *Jordan; Jack Russell Terrier, 12. Loves catching raindrops.*

**8** *Sean Blocksidge*
**8a** *Boef; Border Collie X, 3. Obsessed with big feet.*

**9** *Glen Ryan*
**9a** *Mufasa; Rhodesian Ridgeback, 3. Loves going to work.*

**10** *Tracey Thompson-Bourke*
**10a** *Jasper; Golden Retriever, 8. Loves jumping in puddles.*
**10b** *Jessie; Golden Retriever, 2. Hates rose bushes.*

**11** *Jill Conroy-Welby*
**11a** *Polla; Golden Retriever, 5. Repeat escape artist.*

**MIDGET**

PET HATE: THUNDER
FAVOURITE TOY: ANY STICK
FAVOURITE PASTIME: CATCHING RABBITS
OBSESSIONS: SHEEP, PEOPLE, BIRDS AND HUNTING
NAUGHTIEST DEED: WELCOMING CELLAR DOOR CUSTOMERS WITH A BIG JUMP

| **S KIDMAN WINES** COONAWARRA, SA | BORDER COLLIE, 4 | OWNERS: SUZIE AND SID KIDMAN

FAVOURITE PASTIME: SUNBAKING
OBSESSIONS: SHEEP MUSTERING AND WORKING IN SHEEP YARDS
PET HATES: BEING LEFT ON HER CHAIN FOR MORE THAN AN HOUR
FAVOURITE PASTIME: ROUNDING UP THE CHOOKS AT NIGHT

**PEGGY**

OWNERS: JOHN AND BELINDA THOMSON | KELPIE, 2 | *CRAWFORD RIVER WINES* CONDAH, VIC

COL IS THE WINNER OF THE **'WINE DOGS' INAUGURAL GOLDEN BONE AWARD** FOR BEST BEHAVED WOOFER

*" Don't eat more*
*than you can lift. "*

——— **MISS PIGGY**
*The Muppets*

# Nyam Nyam D. Dog
## CONSULTANT WINE DOG

To:    WINE DOGS
PO BOX 964,
Rozelle NSW 2039
Australia

**RE: NYAM NYAM D. DOG appearing in WINE DOGS**

Dear Wine Dogs,

Thank you for your letter addressed to Nyam Nyam D. Dog, dated 1/9/2004.

As you could well imagine, a basenji with a wine industry and general media profile like Nyam's, is approached hundreds of times, all year long, especially during the course of his 'walkies'.

The vast majority of Nyam Nyam's requests, either by fans, or by numerous business organisations and charities, are sadly declined, due to time constraints and the hectic nature of a dog's life.

Apropos your recent request for Nyam Nyam D. Dog to appear in the second edition of *WINE DOGS: the dogs of the Australasian wineries*, we have some 'issues' to discuss with WINE DOGS, in our capacity as Nyam Nyam's literary and media agents

First and foremost, our client was somewhat perturbed, to put it mildly, not to find the famous 'little basenji with a big bone' on the cover of the first edition of WINE DOGS.

Obviously, we were pleased to hear that you were keen to have Nyam Nyam feature in the second edition. We understand that the star power of a consultant winery dog like Nyam Nyam is bankable, and your request has not been buried.

We're sure you are also well aware of recent tabloid coverage of Nyam, coupled with over-exposure in 'alternative lifestyle' magazines, convincing us that he should return to his vineyard roots, helping restore Nyam Nyam's broad family appeal, whilst also cross-promoting some of his television work on *Bone Idol*, *Boneyard Blitz* and *My Restaurant Bones*.

More so, Nyam is keen to promote his literary career and promote his next book, a self-reverential reference work entitled *The Bitelopedia Nyamtannica*, which has already been commissioned detailing an A to Z of things Nyam Nyam has bitten.

As a consultant winery dog, Nyam Nyam D. Dog has a demanding schedule, often amongst his clients' vineyards and a large number of commercial agreements and sponsorships.

C/O BONE CORPORATION PO BOX 71, STIRLING, ADELAIDE HILLS, SOUTH

Subsequently for Nyam Nyam to appear in your publication a few undertakings are sought, namely;

* Nyam Nyam prefers to work alone and in the past has had 'issues' working with bitzers and will most certainly not work well with cats.

* Please note Nyam Nyam is self-schooled and often chooses not to fetch or sit. He is oft want to express 'I Nyam what I Nyam'.

* Nyam Nyam will only travel first class, on the front seat of the car, with the window partly open. We request no ute trays.

* Nyam Nyam's fees are set on a daily rate and are not negotiable. Bone-based Royalties will be set at 10% of all gross.

* As a devoted 'boneaterian' all his life, Nyam Nyam has specific dietary requirements for the photo shoot.

* With a delicate tan and white coat, Nyam Nyam will provide his own make-up artist.

* Only Agent-approved photographs can be used for the book.

* Lastly, and this is most important, Nyam Nyam will have the final say in what collar he wears and will only consider all natural materials.

I am sure you will agree that Nyam Nyam is a role model for all aspiring winery dogs coming to terms with the fame and fortune that this book will surely thrust upon them.

Nyam Nyam's fame as Wine Dog Consultant came from his role, as a niche market, ancient, African basenji purebreed, making him ideally suited to be a brand name 'ambarkador' for cool climate vineyards working with chardonnay and pinot noir and any bone-dry roses.

In conclusion we have taken the liberty at Bone Corporation of filling in Nyam Nyam's responses to the Wine Dogs questionnaire: *Favourite Toy:* Anything Sheep Skin • *Obsession:* Anything Sheep Skin • *Pet Hates:* Food and wine matching, hippo-infested dams, arising with dignity and Dr Harry • *Naughtiest Deed:* Re-upholstering all soft furnishings for The Bitelopedia Nyamtannica • *Fastest Meal Consumed:* The last one • *Known Accomplices:* His Labrador Agent Polly Waffle D. Dog and brother Taras P. Diddy Dog • *Favourite Pastime:* Sunning himself whilst listening to Wham and the Village People.

Please also find attached a couple of pawed publicity shots.

Thank you again for your enquiry,

Polly Waffle D. Dog,
*Publicist, Bone Corporation.*

All fan mail to: *The Friends of Nyam Nyam M. D. Dog, C/O Bone Corporation, PO Box 71, Stirling, Adelaide Hills, South Australia, 5152 Australia. Email: fans-of-nyam-nyam@strangerandstranger.biz*

POLLY WAFFLE D. DOG WAS AIDED BY SALLY ASHTON AND ZAR BROOKS
SOPHISTS@STRANGERANDSTRANGER.BIZ

OBSESSION: STAFF LUNCH BOXES
NAUGHTIEST DEED: BURYING BONES IN THE VINEYARD
FAVOURITE TOY: THE TELEPHONE
FASTEST MEAL CONSUMED: BOWL OF PRUNES AND FUDGE
KNOWN ACCOMPLICES: NICKY AND MERLOT THE DOG
FAVOURITE COMIC STRIP: FOOTROT FLATS

PADDY

KNOWN ACCOMPLICE: THE CAT
PET HATES: COLD DAYS AND THE CAT
NAUGHTIEST DEED: EATING A MATTRESS
OBSESSION: EATING VINEYARD WORKERS' LUNCHES
FASTEST MEAL CONSUMED: A WHOLE CAMEMBERT
FAVOURITE PASTIME: PATROLLING THE VINEYARD

FAVOURITE TOY: SOCCER BALL
OBSESSION: RIDING THE QUAD BIKE
PET HATE: THE BOARDING KENNELS
KNOWN ACCOMPLICES: SWAN AND NAIK
FAVOURITE PASTIME: LEARNING A FOURTH LANGUAGE

LANCELOT

**SAM**

OBSESSIONS: BALLS, BALLS AND MORE BALLS
NAUGHTIEST DEED: HIDING FROM HIS GROOMER
PET HATE: SUITCASES BEING PACKED
FAVOURITE TOY: WHITE FLUFFY TEDDY BEAR
KNOWN ACCOMPLICES: PX AND RADIGAST

OBSESSION: AVOCADOS
KNOWN ACCOMPLICE: SPOT
PET HATE: GOING TO MILDURA TO HAVE HIS HAIR CUT
FAVOURITE PASTIME: CLEANING OUT THE WINERY BINS
NAUGHTIEST DEED: STEALING THE NEIGHBOUR'S AVOCADOS
AND SNEAKING INTO THEIR HOUSE

TED

**LUCKY**

PET HATE: GUINEA FOWL
FAVOURITE TOY: PILLOWS
FAVOURITE PASTIME: CHASING CROWS AND PARROTS
OBSESSION: BEING IN THE UTE WHEREVER IT GOES
NAUGHTIEST DEED: COCKING HIS LEG ON THE 'WINE DOGS' AUTHOR

**ABBEY VALE** YALLINGUP, WA | KELPIE, 12 | OWNER: PHILIP MAY

PET HATE: TURNING WHEELS
FAVOURITE TOY: BOYD'S LEG
KNOWN ACCOMPLICE: JEDDA
OBSESSION: PEEING IN ALL THE SAME PLACES AS BOYD
FAVOURITE PASTIME: PLAYING WITH HIS BEST MATE JEDDA

PET HATE: DOING WHAT SHE'S TOLD
FASTEST MEAL CONSUMED: ANYTHING YOU'RE EATING
KNOWN ACCOMPLICES: GAIL AND BEAR
FAVOURITE ARTIST: DIANA ROSS

PET HATE: BATHS
KNOWN ACCOMPLICE: SOLOMON
OBSESSIONS: CHASING REFLECTIONS AND SHADOWS
NAUGHTIEST DEED: HOGGING THE BEANBAG IN THE OFFICE
FASTEST MEAL CONSUMED: THE CAT'S FOOD
FAVOURITE PASTIME: CHASING SEAGULLS AT THE BEACH

OBSESSION: BARKING ALL NIGHT WHEN LEFT OUTSIDE
NAUGHTIEST DEED: SLEEPING ON OWNER'S BED DURING THE DAY
PET HATE: BEING LEFT ALONE
FAVOURITE TOYS: SOCKS AND UGH BOOTS
FASTEST MEAL CONSUMED: ANYTHING THAT'S NOT DOG FOOD
KNOWN ACCOMPLICE: FRONTI
FAVOURITE PASTIME: SLEEPING IN THE OFFICE AND SNORING LOUDLY

SOLOMON

*"Everyone's a critic."*

——————— **ANONYMOUS**

# NO DILLYDALLYING
*by Andrew Marsh*

**one of the great features** *of the wine industry is not what is necessarily in the bottle, nor is it the flamboyancy and showmanship of the people involved. It rests on a hairy-looking creature that lurks around vineyards and cellar doors and wineries. It is, of course, the winery dog. They are the backbone of our industry. Always around, always reliable, always lovable. Most take their names from grape varieties or famous wine labels or industry identities. Some even go so far as to use wine "God" titles.*

*All I know is that many wineries in the world can't function without them. They are far from simple pets. They are part of the winegrowing and winemaking process. You often view them strutting around the cellar door as though they own the place. They'll greet you in the carpark and entice you in – "Hey there, that's right, a little pat, that's it, check the collar, that's my name. OK, everyone follow me, c'mon now, no dillydallying (why do they always dillydally?). That's right, gather round and I'll get someone over here to ... Hey, keep paying me attention. Just 'cause I wasn't blessed with four fingers and an opposable thumb to pour wine in your glass doesn't mean I'm not still the centrepiece ... c'mon now, look at me."*

*Winery dogs come in all shapes and sizes, colours and creeds. As so often happens they can mimic their owner's behaviour and often grow to look similar. If you walk into many wineries in Germany you will certainly see what I mean. A huge German with a handle-bar moustache will be standing behind a bar snorting and wheezing as*

*he tries to perform the most effortless tasks and seated at the end of the long bar will be a massive St Bernard, snorting and wheezing and dribbling everywhere.*

*In Spain last year I visited a winery where a little obstacle course was made for the winery chihuahua. He ends the course running up a series of flights of stairs on the winery wall and activates a gravity-fed valve which releases a nip of sherry that winds its way down a clear hose. You stand there with your glass under the end to receive the sherry sample, take a tiny biscuit from the bowl sitting next to you and reward the dog who has since slid down a little slippery dip to meet you. Poor little thing was exhausted by the time I had finished tasting.*

*So whenever you find yourself in the great wine regions of the world, take heed of the real winemaster, and remember ... no dillydallying!*

ANDREW MARSH IS WINEMAKER AT MARSH ESTATE, POKOLBIN, NSW.

PET HATE: PUPPIES
NAUGHTIEST DEED: STEALING CHOCOLATE BARS
FAVOURITE JOB: SHIFTING BOULDERS
FAVOURITE PASTIME: EXPLORING RUGGED TERRAIN
OBSESSION: TRYING TO MOVE LOGS AS IF THEY WERE STICKS

SPIKE

PET HATE: BEING LEFT ALONE
KNOWN ACCOMPLICE: OSCAR
FAVOURITE TOYS: TENNIS BALLS AND MONTY THE RAT
FAVOURITE PASTIME: BEING TAKEN FOR LONG WALKS
NAUGHTIEST DEED: CLIMBING ONTO THE ROOF IN POURING RAIN

**SALTRAM** ANGASTON, SA | LABRADOR / RETRIEVER X, 3 | OWNER: NIGEL DOLAN

OBSESSION: BEGGING AT TABLES
NAUGHTIEST DEED: ATE TWO NEW AKUBRA HATS
PET HATE: GETTING WASHED
FAVOURITE TOY: FOOD
KNOWN ACCOMPLICES: GUESTS AT THE RESTAURANT

MAX

OBSESSIONS: SHEEP AND DUCKS
NAUGHTIEST DEED: PARTIAL TO POULTRY
PET HATE: DAYS OFF – BORN TO WORK (STILL ON P PLATES)
FASTEST MEAL CONSUMED: LEFTOVERS
KNOWN ACCOMPLICES: TALLY AND BRODY

JOCK

| **STANTON AND KILLEEN** RUTHERGLEN, VIC | BORDER COLLIE X, 1 | OWNERS: CHRIS AND ANN KILLEEN

MISHA

OBSESSION: CHASING KANGAROOS
FAVOURITE TOY: A 'TUGGER'
FASTEST MEAL CONSUMED: SCHMACKOS
KNOWN ACCOMPLICE: PANDA
NAUGHTIEST DEED: EATING IRRIGATION PIPES
FAVOURITE PASTIME: GREETING CUSTOMERS AT THE CELLAR DOOR

PANDA

PET HATE: THE VET
FAVOURITE TOY: MISHA
KNOWN ACCOMPLICE: MISHA
NAUGHTIEST DEED: SWIMMING IN THE DAM AFTER BATHS
OBSESSION: BEING LOVED BY EVERYONE

FAVOURITE TOY: OLD SHOES
OBSESSION: GREETING VISITORS WITH A SHOE
NAUGHTIEST DEED: TEARING APART CUSHIONS
PET HATES: TRACTORS AND VACUUM CLEANERS
FASTEST MEAL CONSUMED: CHICKEN NECKS
KNOWN ACCOMPLICE: ZENA
FAVOURITE PASTIME: HANGING AROUND JAMES

SKYE

154   **TALIJANCICH WINES** HERNE HILL, WA | GOLDEN RETRIEVER, 2 | OWNER: JAMES TALIJANCICH

OBSESSION: SQUEAKY TOYS
PET HATES: WATER AND THUNDER
FASTEST MEAL CONSUMED: ROAST LAMB
FAVOURITE PASTIME: GOING TO THE BEACH
NAUGHTIEST DEED: BURYING ELAINE'S SHOES WHEN LEFT BEHIND

OWNER: ELAINE BARRY | GERMAN SHEPHERD/RIDGEBACK X, 8 | AQUILA ESTATE CARABOOD | 157

**LOUIS**

OBSESSION: FOOD
PET HATE: BEING LEFT ALONE
FAVOURITE TOY: SKULLY (SOFT TOY FROM MONSTERS INC)
NAUGHTIEST DEED: HIDING BILL'S UNDERPANTS UNDER THE CUPBOARD
FAVOURITE PASTIME: CUDDLING ANNA

ALLANDALE WINERY, LOVEDALE, NSW | LABRADOR, 15 WEEKS | OWNER: ANNA SNEDDON (PICTURED)

OBSESSION: AVID DUCK WATCHER
NAUGHTIEST DEED: CHEWING A CANE CHAIR
PET HATE:  THE NATIONAL ANTHEM
FASTEST MEAL CONSUMED: FRIED EGGS
KNOWN ACCOMPLICE: HER SISTER MAX
FAVOURITE PASTIME: CHIEF OF HOUSEHOLD SECURITY

FINN

MAX

OBSESSION: DEVOTED CHICKEN WATCHER
NAUGHTIEST DEED: ATE FIRST DOG BED
PET HATE: THE WOOFA WASH HAIR DRYER
FASTEST MEAL CONSUMED: FILLET STEAK
KNOWN ACCOMPLICE: HER SISTER FINN
FAVOURITE PASTIME: VINEYARD SUPERVISOR

**THE LANE VINEYARDS** HAHNDORF, SA | BORDER COLLIE, 2 | OWNER: HELEN EDWARDS

OBSESSION: RABBITS
PET HATE: HELICOPTERS
FAVOURITE TOY: BOOT TAGS
FASTEST MEAL CONSUMED: TIM TAMS
NAUGHTIEST DEED: BRINGING HOME A DEAD CARP
KNOWN ACCOMPLICES: JACK AND JILL THE JACK RUSSELLS
FAVOURITE PASTIME: RIDING ON THE MOTORBIKE

BLOSSOM

**RUBY RED**

OBSESSION: STICKS
NAUGHTIEST DEED: PUTTING STICKS ON PEOPLE'S SHOES
PET HATE: WINDY NIGHTS
FAVOURITE TOY: STICKS
FASTEST MEAL CONSUMED: CHICKEN NECKS
KNOWN ACCOMPLICE: TRUE BLUE

MT LOFTY RANGES VINEYARD, LENSWOOD, SA | QUEENSLAND HEELER, 4 | OWNERS: ALAN HERATH AND IAN REE

OBSESSION: STICKS
NAUGHTIEST DEED: PRUNING YOUNG VINES
PET HATE: HOT AIR BALLOONS
FAVOURITE TOY: ANY STICK
FAVOURITE PASTIME: BARKING AT PASSING CARS

TEAL

TOMMY

PET HATE: *BEING LEFT OUT*
OBSESSION: *BEING SPIRITUAL*
NAUGHTIEST DEED: *EATING ALAN'S GUMBOOTS*
FASTEST MEAL CONSUMED: *BREAKFAST AND DINNER*

**STONECROFT** HASTINGS, NZ │ BOXER, 7 │ OWNER: ALAN LIMMER (PICTURED)

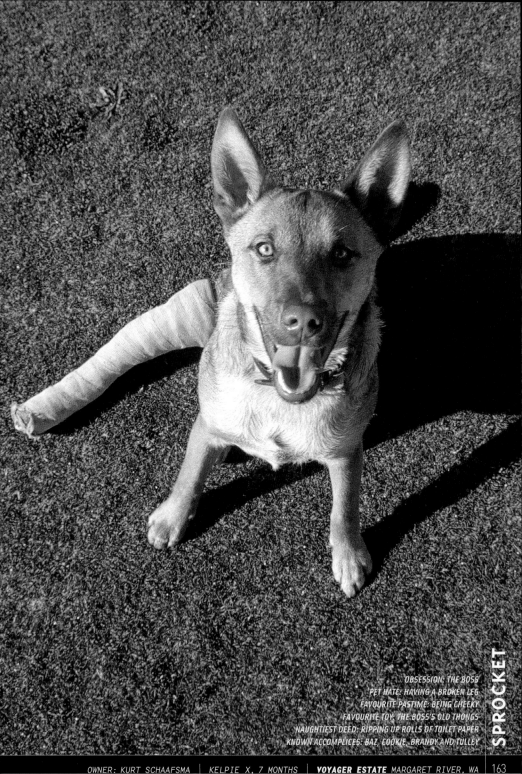

OBSESSION: THE BOSS
PET HATE: HAVING A BROKEN LEG
FAVOURITE PASTIME: BEING CHEEKY
FAVOURITE TOY: THE BOSS'S OLD THONGS
NAUGHTIEST DEED: RIPPING UP ROLLS OF TOILET PAPER
KNOWN ACCOMPLICES: BAZ, COOKIE, BRANDY AND TULLEY

SPROCKET

OWNER: KURT SCHAAFSMA | KELPIE X, 7 MONTHS | **VOYAGER ESTATE** MARGARET RIVER, WA | 163

OBSESSION: BREAKFAST BONE
PET HATE: KANGAROOS
FAVOURITE TOY: DOG BISCUITS
FASTEST MEAL CONSUMED: TINNED FOOD
KNOWN ACCOMPLICES: MONTY AND BAXTER
FAVOURITE PASTIME: BEING WITH JUDITH ON THE QUAD BIKE

PET HATE: TRACTORS
OBSESSION: G-STRINGS
FASTEST MEAL CONSUMED: WHOLE CHEESE PLATTER
KNOWN ACCOMPLICES: ELIZA AND PETER BROWN
FAVOURITE PASTIME: RUNNING ALONG THE MURRAY RIVER
NAUGHTIEST DEED: DRAGGING OUT ELIZA'S UNDERWEAR ON FIRST DATES

VINO

OWNER: ELIZA BROWN (PICTURED) | GERMAN SHEPHERD, 4 MONTHS | **ALL SAINTS ESTATE** WAHGUNYAH, VIC | 165

MAYNARD

FAVOURITE TOY: AUSSIE RULES FOOTY
KNOWN ACCOMPLICE: BOOPH
FAVOURITE PASTIME: UNOFFICIAL PATRON
OF HARRIGAN'S PUB

**TOWER ESTATE** POKOLBIN, NSW | BLUE HEELER, 10 | OWNER: DAN DINEEN

FAVOURITE TOY: THE HOSE
FAVOURITE PASTIME: SWIMMING
OBSESSIONS: MICE AND DIGGING HOLES
PET HATE: BEING LEFT OUT OF THE ACTION
FAVOURITE TOY: THE 4-WHEEL MOTORBIKE
FAVOURITE JOB: ROUNDING UP SHEEP
KNOWN ACHIEVEMENTS: THE SECOND LAW OF THERMODYNAMICS

MOG

*"Outside of a dog, a book
is man's best friend. Inside of
a dog it's too hard to read."*

—————— GROUCHO MARX

# MAYNARD'S SHOUT!

*by Andrew Marsh*

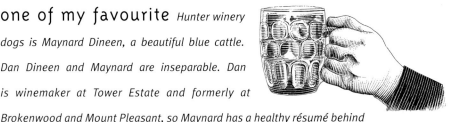

**one of my favourite** *Hunter winery dogs is Maynard Dineen, a beautiful blue cattle. Dan Dineen and Maynard are inseparable. Dan is winemaker at Tower Estate and formerly at* Brokenwood and Mount Pleasant, so Maynard has a healthy résumé behind him. After work, Dan used to enjoy a refreshment or two at the old Tallawanta Hotel. Each day, Dan would sternly tell Maynard to stay put at the front door of the pub as he walked in with a stubby of Melbourne Bitter. Don't worry, all the crew at Brokenwood would be armed with a stubby upon entering the old Tallawanta. Part of the uniform. Maynard didn't like missing out on all the action and would try anything to join in, such as push his face against the window and force out sulky barks.

After a while Maynard became fed up with having to hang outside while his best mate enjoyed the comforts of cold beer and air-conditioning. After all, he was a winery dog, one of the crew. He'd been up at the crack of dawn rounding up tractors, motivating the staff, entertaining potential buyers and generally keeping an eye (and a nose) on things. So began the practice of slyly tiptoeing into the pub as the door was randomly opened by incoming or outgoing patrons. Maynard would peek around the corner, spot Dan at the far end of the bar and while Dan had his head turned, would dash over to the beer trough (the trough which runs along the bottom of the bar) and proceed with great caution. It was funny seeing this sissy cattle dog trying ever so shrewdly to quietly make his way along the narrow v-shaped trough.

*Eventually Maynard would make it all the way to the end of the bar and if no-one was cruel enough to alarm Dan that he had sneaked in, Maynard would stand in the trough or sit under Dan's seat for several minutes before being caught. "Out" would come the cry from Master Dan as he guided Maynard out the door ... "STAY!"*

*Within minutes Maynard would be back, then out again, then back again. This was a continuous cycle. One particularly busy Friday night Dan was called away from the pub to attend to something back at work. He informed a small group of us to make sure Maynard stayed outside and behaved himself. About ten minutes later there was a huge bang and screams from a group of young, glitzy-looking girls who were seated along the bar. There was a huge commotion. Dust seemed to be flying everywhere, drinks were dropped, sending smashed glass across the bar floor and one of the girls was lying on her back covered in beer.*

*Some people debate what actually happened that night but I saw the entire episode unfold before my very own eyes. Maynard had sneaked in and was making his way along a very full and very smelly beer trough. Someone had thrown a partly empty packet of twisties into the trough, which Maynard had stuck his nose into. He was really tackling this packet and I seemed to notice he was struggling to take his snout out of it. As he was wrestling with the bag he brushed up against the legs of one of the girls who was taken by surprise, letting out a sharp scream and dropping the cigarette and drink in her hand onto poor Maynard. Suffering a little shock himself, Maynard stopped in his tracks, completely unaware that he was now standing on the burning cigarette, having lodged up into his paw.*

*"BANG!" Maynard jumped three feet, hit his head under the bar and then shot out sideways, yelping in agony and sending one of the girls mid-air and onto the ground. Mounds of cigarette ash filled the air from the trough and broken glass shattered everywhere. It all happened so quickly. The bar looked like a bombsite.*

*Maynard shot off outside. Dan arrived back shortly after things had settled down tagging with him a very sorry-looking canine. Maynard was covered head to toe in spilt beer, cigarette ash and odd bits of different rubbish that had stuck to his coat. His face was covered in yellow goo from the twisties and he was sporting a new limp. If he had a girlfriend dog he'd be in all sorts of trouble. "I better let him stay inside the pub tonight" explained a very puzzled Dan. "Did you guys see anything, or hear anything? He looks like he's been in a fight or something." "No ... nah ... not that I can recall ... no, nothing" we replied. One of the girls then came gushing over "Oh, poor puppy dog, are you OK? Is your footsie alrigggght? You're a naughty boy but you're sooooo cute..." Dan looked straight back at us. "Oh, come to think of it, there was one small incident ..."*

IN MEMORY OF SPUNKY MARSH 1982 – 93.

ANDREW MARSH IS WINEMAKER AT MARSH ESTATE, POKOLBIN, NSW.

MOLLY

KNOWN ACCOMPLICE: JACKO
NAUGHTIEST DEED: STEALING SAUSAGES
PET HATES: LULU THE CAT AND JET PLANES
FAVOURITE TOY: A SQUEAKY BOXING GLOVE
FAVOURITE PASTIME: CHASING HIGH-SPEED SOCCER BALLS
OBSESSION: RIDING WITH HER HEAD OUTSIDE THE CAR WINDOW

**JACKSON ESTATE** MARLBOROUGH, NZ | BEARDED JACK RUSSELL TERRIER, 2 | OWNERS: JO AND JOHN STICHBUR

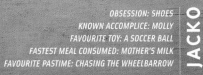

OBSESSION: SHOES
KNOWN ACCOMPLICE: MOLLY
FAVOURITE TOY: A SOCCER BALL
FASTEST MEAL CONSUMED: MOTHER'S MILK
FAVOURITE PASTIME: CHASING THE WHEELBARROW

JACKO

CABERNET

OBSESSION: BITING TRACTOR TYRES
PET HATE: THUNDERSTORMS
FAVOURITE TOY: IRIS'S BED
KNOWN ACCOMPLICES: IRIS AND THE CATS
FAVOURITE PASTIME: SLEEPING IN THE TRUCK
NAUGHTIEST DEED: STEALING A LEG OF LAMB FROM THE KITCHEN BENCH

**MIRAMAR WINES** MUDGEE, NSW | BORDER COLLIE, 9 | OWNER: IAN MACRAE

OBSESSION: BEING ADMIRED
NAUGHTIEST DEED: EATING THE WORKERS' LUNCH
PET HATE: BEING KICKED OFF THE LOUNGE
KNOWN ACCOMPLICES: CABERNET AND PERCY
FAVOURITE PASTIME: RECEIVING THE ADORATION OF THE CUSTOMERS

IRIS

**JENNA**

PET HATE: BEING CLEAN
OBSESSION: STACKING KIDS ON BIKES
FAVOURITE TOY: THE METER READER
FASTEST MEAL CONSUMED: DUCK EGGS
KNOWN ACCOMPLICE: APRIL THE GOAT
FAVOURITE MOVIE: DOG DAY AFTERNOON

**HARBORD WINES** STOCKWELL, SA | DALMATIAN, 13 | OWNER: ROGER HARBORD

OBSESSION: *HERDING THE UTE*
NAUGHTIEST DEED: *CHEWING UP NEW ADIDAS TRAINERS*
PET HATE: *MAGPIES THAT FILCH FROM HIS BOWL*
FAVOURITE TOY: *VINE PRUNINGS*
FASTEST MEAL CONSUMED: *PORK SAUSAGE*
KNOWN ACCOMPLICE: *NERO*

**BACCHUS**

JIMMY

OBSESSION: SWIMMING IN THE SEA
NAUGHTIEST DEED: CHASING BIRDS
FAVOURITE TOY: ROLY
KNOWN ACCOMPLICE: TOLERATING ROLY
FAVOURITE PASTIMES: CHASING SEAGULLS AND RUNNING ON THE BEACH

**HUGH HAMILTON WINES** McLAREN VALE, SA | LABRADOR / KELPIE X, 9 | OWNER: PAM HAMILTON

OBSESSION: PLAYING FOOTBALL
NAUGHTIEST DEED: PEEING ON BARRELS
PET HATES: BLACKBIRDS AND INDIAN MYNAHS
FAVOURITE TOY: OSSO BUCO BONE
KNOWN ACCOMPLICE: BOUCHON THE CAT
FASTEST MEAL CONSUMED: BLUE CHEESE AND CHICKEN BONES
FAVOURITE PASTIME: GETTING THAI MASSAGES FROM VINEYARD WORKERS

BRUNO

OWNER: PHILLIP JONES | KELPIE X, 8 | **BASS PHILLIP WINES** LEONGATHA SOUTH, VIC | 179

## BONNY

NAUGHTIEST DEED: ROLLING IN SHEEP POO
PET HATES: WILD CATS, FERRETS AND BIRDS
KNOWN ACCOMPLICE: BURG THE POODLE
FAVOURITE PASTIME: HANGING OUT IN THE OFFICE
OBSESSION: SNEAKING ONTO BEDS IN THE MIDDLE OF THE NIGHT

**MURDOCH JAMES ESTATE** MARTINBOROUGH, NZ | LABRADOR / TERRIER X, 8 | OWNER: JAMES WALKER

**BACI**

OBSESSION: MILK
NAUGHTIEST DEED: SLEEPING ON TOP OF OTHER PUPPIES
PET HATE: HAVING NINE BROTHERS AND SISTERS
FASTEST MEAL CONSUMED: MILK
FAVOURITE PASTIME: SLEEPING

**CEILIDH**

OBSESSION: CHASING ANYTHING THAT MOVES
NAUGHTIEST DEED: CHEWING A HOLE IN THE LOUNGEROOM CARPET
PET HATE: NOT BEING THE CENTRE OF ATTENTION
KNOWN ACCOMPLICE: 'REBEL' OLIVER
FAVOURITE PASTIME: BEING THE CENTRE OF ATTENTION

OWNER: ALASDAIR AND TRISH SUTHERLAND | LABRADOR, 2 | **CAPERCAILLE WINE** LOVEDALE, NSW | 183

OBSESSION: BIRDS
NAUGHTIEST DEED: DIGGING HOLES
PET HATE: BATHS
FAVOURITE TOYS: BALLS, BONES AND SHOES
FASTEST MEAL CONSUMED: EVERY ONE
FAVOURITE PASTIMES: EATING, SLEEPING AND CHASING BIRDS

BRISTOL FARM MAIN RIDGE VIC | GOLDEN RETRIEVER 6 | OWNERS: WAYNE AND CAROL CONDON

BAZIL BROWN

PET HATE: TOENAILS BEING CUT
FAVOURITE TOY: GRAPE VINES CUTTINGS
FAVOURITE PASTIMES: CHASING BIRDS AND BEING PATTED
OBSESSION: MARKING EVERY TYRE ON VISITORS' CARS

OWNERS: DARREN AND JAC

*"The reason a dog has so many
friends is that he wags his tail
instead of his tongue."*

—————— **ANONYMOUS**

# FROM THE DOG'S MOUTH

*by Phil Laing*

PHIL LAING, AUTHOR OF *TASMANIAN WINES* AND CONTRIBUTOR TO *AUSTRALIAN VIGNERONS AND NATIONAL GRAPEGROWERS*, GAINED AN EXCLUSIVE INTERVIEW WITH TASMANIAN VINEYARD DOG OF THE YEAR, **BAZIL BROWN** OF PUDDLEDUCK VINEYARD.

*Bazil, what do you view as the critical aspects of the vineyard dog role?*

It begins in the vineyard and carries through all aspects of wine production to cellar door sales. Vineyard managers will tell you that great wine is made in the vineyard, winemakers will tell you that what happens in the winery is the crucial input, sales and marketing say their work is indispensable. But they'll all agree that the vineyard dog is the one who brings everything together and provides the necessary links and continuity.

*How did you get started in the wine industry?*

My father was an Australian champion, but that wasn't the show circuit I chose as a career. As a puppy I began an apprenticeship with Darren, accompanying him around the vineyards, the winery and cellar door. Being able to work in a number of different vineyards and swap information with colleagues provided me with a wealth of information. I'm now available in a consulting role, to pass on the knowledge and experience I've acquired.

*What initially attracted you to the job?*

Working outdoors has great appeal and there is always plenty to do. I love going to work each day. Plus I have an important staff morale role, continually going up and down the rows encouraging the workers through long days of picking, then months of pruning.

### Which is the most demanding time of the year?

*Late summer and early autumn, once you have veraison until the grapes are picked. The birds are part of the biodiversity of the vineyard but once they get a taste of the ripe fruit they become a real problem and you have your work cut out.*

### Who are your heroes or role models?

*The very first vineyard dog in Tasmania was Rex at Prospect Farm on Newtown Rivulet, just a couple of kilometres upstream on the Derwent River from Hobart Town in the 1820s. A real pioneer who faced the challenges of cool climate viticulture in a new and often harsh environment, he is a historical figure who is a real inspiration to us all.*

The facts are obscured by time but Rex seems to have disappeared to the Victorian goldfields around 1850, along with other vineyard dogs of the time, and the early Tasmanian industry withered.

### Any other historical figures?

In the re-establishment of the industry in the late 1950s there was the dalmatian dynasty of Moorilla Estate, on the banks of the Derwent just a little further upriver than Prospect Farm. The founder was Sacha, her daughter was Leisle and her grandson Andy; and there was Chloe, another dalmatian. In the north of the State there was a French dog in the 1950s at La Provence, and then Frank the labrador put Pipers Brook on the map with its vineyard established in the 1970s and production in the '80s.

### Who are the modern role models?

In recent times Trooper the golden retriever at Craigie Knowe on the east coast was the inaugural winner of the Tasmanian Vineyard Dog of the Year Award. The second recipient was Jacko the Jack Russell of Elsewhere Vineyard in the Huon Valley. Jacko, although officially retired at No Regrets, is still growing pinot noir and enjoys a glass or two.

### How important is your cellar door and customer relations role?

It is vital for the long-term viability of the enterprise. For many visitors, who are all potential customers, the first contact is with the vineyard dog in the car park. That initial impression is so important. I make a point of leaving my signature on each and every tyre as a memento for the visitors to take away with them.

### Is it fair to say that, as one of the few corgis in the wine industry, you also are an inspiration to others of your breed?

The wine industry has been dominated traditionally by border collies, Jack Russells, labradors and retrievers. Although corgis were originally working dogs, the royal 'chardonnay pack' has given us a different public image. I hope I've been able to pioneer a path for young corgis to follow.

*What are the natural advantages for you and your breed?*

*Being very low strung we can run at full speed under the bottom wire. The dripper line is at eye height and so we are the logical choice to be put in charge of the irrigation system. I'm also the perfect height for registering the tyres of visitors' vehicles. Being close to the ground also keeps us aware of vineyard diseases and pests.*

*You are often seen making the smallest of holes bigger and eventually disappearing down them. What's the science behind this?*

*I've developed an appreciation of terroir and the role of soil science. My home vineyard, Puddleduck on the banks of Stoney Creek, is sandy loam with pebbles and some quartz.*

*And your favourite wine?*

*Call me parochial or say I've got to confess to a cellar palate, but I've developed a real thirst for the wines of the Coal River Valley.*

*Favourite food?*

*Wallaby, rabbit, anything with "Get the …" in front of it.*

PET HATE: FERAL CATS
FAVOURITE TOY: ROZ'S PET FERRET, SACRED
OBSESSION: TEARING UP CARTONS OF WINE
FASTEST MEAL CONSUMED: LUMIERE'S FOOD
KNOWN ACCOMPLICE: LUMIERE THE WHITE CAT
FAVOURITE PASTIME: JUMPING FENCES AT A SINGLE BOUND
NAUGHTIEST DEED: HIDE AND SEEK IN THE SUPERMARKET

**LUNA**

**LUCA**

OBSESSION: *RIDING IN THE BACK OF UTES*
NAUGHTIEST DEED: *ROLLING IN DEAD THINGS*
PET HATE: *BEING VACUUM CLEANED*
FAVOURITE TOY: *HILUX UTE*
FASTEST MEAL CONSUMED: *FILLET STEAK FROM GUEST'S PLATE*
KNOWN ACCOMPLICE: *FLAT THE SHED CAT*

**LEO BURING** EDEN VALLEY, SA | AUSTRALIAN CATTLE DOG, 6 | OWNER: GREG PEARCE

OBSESSION: CHEWING CHILDREN'S TOYS AND SPRINKLERS
NAUGHTIEST DEED: COLLECTING AND EATING FREE RANGE EGGS
PET HATE: BEING RESTRAINED
FAVOURITE TOY: EVERYTHING PLASTIC
FAVOURITE PASTIME: GUARDING THE HOUSE

CODY

SIMBA

PET HATE: FLIES
OBSESSION: CHASING POSSUMS
NAUGHTIEST DEED: JUMPING IN THE DAM JUST BEFORE GOING HOME
FAVOURITE TOY: STUFFED TOYS THAT MAKE A NOISE
KNOWN ACCOMPLICES: JAZZ AND DRUM

PET HATE: *THE VACUUM CLEANER*
FAVOURITE TOY: *LEATHER GLOVES*
NAUGHTIEST DEED: *DESTROYING POT PLANTS*
FAVOURITE PASTIME: *VINEYARD MANAGEMENT*
KNOWN ACCOMPLICES: *WALLY NEXT DOOR, UNCLE SAM AND COUSIN SIMBA*
OBSESSION: *CHASING AIR LINES THROUGH THE VINEYARD AS THEY'RE ROLLED UP*

JAZZ

# TWIGGY

OBSESSION: WATER HOSE
PET HATE: CYCLISTS
FAVOURITE TOY: ANY PLASTIC BOTTLE
FAVOURITE FRUIT: RIESLING GRAPES
(DOESN'T LIKE OTHER VARIETIES)
FAVOURITE PASTIME: LYING IN THE SUN
NAUGHTIEST DEED: TAKING SCHMACKOS
OUT OF THE AUTHOR'S POCKET

**FREYCINET VINEYARDS** BICHENO, TAS | HEELER/WHIPPET X, 2 | OWNER: PAULA KLOOSTERMAN

SASSOON

OBSESSION: RETRIEVING
FAVOURITE TOY: A SMALL KEN DOLL THAT BEARS A STRIKING
RESEMBLANCE TO A WELL-KNOWN AUSTRALIAN WINE WRITER
FASTEST MEAL CONSUMED: THERE ISN'T A STOPWATCH FAST ENOUGH

**OLIVER**

PET HATE: VACUUM CLEANERS
KNOWN ACCOMPLICE: SKIPPER
OBSESSION: TAKING A BISCUIT TO BED
FAVOURITE TOY: YELLOW RUBBER HEDGEHOG
NAUGHTIEST DEED: ESCAPING THROUGH LAUNDRY WINDOW
FAVOURITE PASTIME: CHASING RUNDLE, HUTT AND CARRINGTON

198 | **MALCOLM CREEK VINEYARD** KERSBROOK, SA | FOX TERRIER X, 5 | OWNERS: REG AND LIZ TOLLEY

OBSESSION: CHASING AWAY THE SPOOKS
PET HATE: NOT BEING ALLOWED IN THE CAFÉ
KNOWN ACCOMPLICES: DIRK, TIPSY, DOLLY, MAYNARD AND BOOPH
FAVOURITE PASTIME: PLAYING RACETRACKS WITH DIRK
NAUGHTIEST DEED: TRYING TO FLY JOHN SINGLETON'S HELICOPTER

BULA

**BECKIE**

OBSESSION: BEING PART OF THE VINEYARD ACTION
NAUGHTIEST DEED: OCCASIONALLY OVEREATING
KNOWN ACCOMPLICE: AUNT JESS
FAVOURITE PASTIME: MEETING PEOPLE
FASTEST MEAL CONSUMED: THE DAY THE FREEZER WAS CLEANED OUT
PET HATE: MAGPIES ON PRINCIPLE – RESENTS THE FACT THAT SHE HAS NEVER CAUGHT ONE

PARADISE ENOUGH WINES KONGWAK, VIC | NEW ZEALAND BORDER COLLIE, 12 | OWNERS: JOHN BELL AND FAMILY

KNOWN ACCOMPLICE: SAM
PET HATE: NOT BEING AT WORK
OBSESSION: BALLS, BALLS AND MORE BALLS
NAUGHTIEST DEED: THE ODD CRUTCH SNIFF
FAVOURITE TOY: ANY ROUND OBJECT AS LONG AS IT ROLLS
FAVOURITE PASTIME: ANTI-SEAGULL PATROL

MAX

OWNER: COLIN RAYMENT | BORDER COLLIE X, 9 | KAY'S AMERY WINERY McLAREN VALE, SA

**BERT**

PET HATE: *HOSES*
OBSESSION: *PEEING ON CAR TYRES*
KNOWN ACCOMPLICE: *WALDO*

**CLOUDY BAY** *BLENHEIM, NZ* | *LABRADOR, 2* | *OWNER: JEREMY WATTS*

OBSESSIONS: POPPY AND RABBITS
NAUGHTIEST DEED: EATING EVERYTHING
PET HATES: THE COLD AND LOUD TRACTORS
FAVOURITE TOY: DI'S HIGH-HEELED SHOES
FASTEST MEAL CONSUMED: DI'S SUNGLASSES
KNOWN ACCOMPLICES: BELLA AND HOUGHSTON

FAVOURITE TOY: HONEY
PET HATE: LATE DINNERS
OBSESSION: BREAKING LAND SPEED RECORDS
FAVOURITE PASTIME: SMELLING FOR RABBITS

**HARRIET**

*OBSESSION: BITING MALE VISITORS*
*NAUGHTIEST DEED: MADE A MEAL OF AN ORTHODONTIC PLATE*
*PET HATE: THE MAILMAN*
*FAVOURITE TOY: 4-WHEEL MOTORBIKE*
*FASTEST MEAL CONSUMED: WEETBIX AND MILK*
*KNOWN ACCOMPLICE: DEANIE*

**DAPHNE**

*OBSESSION: BARKING*
*FAVOURITE TOY: 4-WHEEL MOTORBIKE*
*FASTEST MEAL CONSUMED: EMU EGG*
*FAVOURITE PASTIME: HOWLING AT THE TELEPHONE*
*PET HATE: BEING HOME ALONE WHEN THE BIKE IS GONE*

**CANONBAH BRIDGE** WARREN, NSW | SEALYHAM TERRIER, 4 (LEFT) AND NZ HUNTERAWAY, 5 (MIDDLE)

PET HATE: MALE VISITORS
FAVOURITE TOY: 4-WHEEL MOTORBIKE
KNOWN ACCOMPLICES: HARRIET AND DAPHNE
FAVOURITE PASTIME: WINNING DOG RACES AT NYNGAN SHOW
OBSESSION: CHASING ECHIDNAS THAT LIVE UNDER THE VERANDAH

DEANIE

**PINOT**

OBSESSION: THE MITCHELL FAMILY
NAUGHTIEST DEED: SWIMMING AFTER A LARGE SEAL
PET HATE: BEING CONFINED
FAVOURITE TOY: HIS SISTER ROSE
KNOWN ACCOMPLICE: HIS COUSIN WILLOW
FAVOURITE PASTIME: SNIFFING OUT THINGS TO CHASE

| **MONTALTO VINEYARDS** RED HILL SOUTH, VIC | SNOODLE, 2 | OWNERS: JOHN AND WENDY MITCHELL

PET HATE: PEOPLE WITH FACIAL HAIR
NAUGHTIEST DEED: CONTROLLING GUINEA FOWL POPULATION
KNOWN ACCOMPLICE: PREVIOUSLY KIMBA, THE WHITE LAB
FAVOURITE PASTIMES: WALKING AND HAVING COMPANY

OWNER: PHILIP MAY | KELPIE, 12 | **ABBEY VALE** YALLINGUP, WA

*"To love one's self is the beginning
of a life-long romance."*

——————— **OSCAR WILDE**

# INSPECTOR **MAX**

*by Lisa McGuigan*

## Growing up in the Hunter Valley *at*

*Wyndham Estate, dogs had always been an important part of my life. We shared our house with two much-loved labradors who epitomised the concept of a wine dog: they were named Hermitage and TR2, after my father Brian McGuigan's most successful wines of the time.*

*A decade later after travelling the world and a hospitality career in Sydney, I moved back to the Hunter Valley to set up Hunter Cellars and my love of dogs was re-ignited. It wasn't long before Max, a German shepherd of formidable size, had become a regular fixture in my life. I always loved big dogs, which were completely out of the question for me when I lived in the city. When I moved back to the country, getting a dog was my top priority and size was not an issue.*

*My red sports car was sidelined for a cumbersome four-wheel drive and my neat freak nature was forced to make concessions for the trail of long hair that followed me everywhere, manifesting itself on every item of black clothing and furniture I owned.*

*The choice of a German shepherd was in part influenced by my desire for a sense of security. I was living alone when I first moved back to the country and worked late into the night for the first few months setting up the Cellar. Max proved to be the perfect guard dog. Like any good wine dog, Max had the most incredible nose. I used to tell bus groups that he was trained to sniff out wine bottles and that he would frisk people if necessary. They knew I was kidding but theft dropped dramatically as a result.*

*After dark, Max's guard dog skills came to the fore and he would become very protective of me with all evening visitors. However, his hospitality skills left a little to be desired. One particular incident was a visit by an international VIP that had been carefully orchestrated for months. They arrived in the early evening for a private tasting, followed by dinner. Everything was planned with military precision, except for one uncontrollable detail. When they arrived, Max wouldn't let them out of the car. Positioning himself with his paws on the roof of the car and his head in the window, he barked away fiercely. But old Max's bark was much worse than his bite as he was very much a gentle giant. A quick mobile call to me and I went outside to rescue my guests. Max and my guests quickly warmed to each other and a memorable night was had by all.*

*Max was a superb wine dog and even better security dog.*

LISA McGUIGAN IS GENERAL MANAGER OF TEMPUS TWO WINES.

OBSESSION: DIGGING HOLES
FAVOURITE TOY: ABEL THE CAT
PET HATE: THE RUBBISH COLLECTORS
FASTEST MEAL CONSUMED: STOLEN PORK CHOPS
FAVOURITE PASTIME: ROLLING IN DEAD POSSUMS
NAUGHTIEST DEED: ROAMING THE VINEYARD AND ORCHARDS
KNOWN ACCOMPLICES: ANNABEL, JOSEFIEN, RUTGER, RUUD AND DORIEN

ROSIE

CANDY

OBSESSIONS: BEING NICK'S SHADOW AND THE CATS
PET HATE: THE VET
KNOWN ACCOMPLICE: CINDY
FAVOURITE PASTIME: HANGING OUT WITH OTHER DOGS

**GREVILLEA ESTATE** *BEGA, NSW* | *LABRADOR, 1* | *OWNER: NICKY COLLINS*

OBSESSION: THUNDER
NAUGHTIEST DEED: GRABBING PASTA FROM THE PANTRY
PET HATE: GROOMING AT THE PET PARLOUR
FAVOURITE TOY: MOTHER'S BLACK UNDERWEAR
KNOWN ACCOMPLICE: CHARLIE
FAVOURITE PASTIME: WATCHING OLD MOVIES ON TV

OBSESSION: FERAL CATS
PET HATE: BEING FLUFFED AT THE GROOMERS
FAVOURITE TOY: FATHER'S BEANIE
FASTEST MEAL CONSUMED: CHEESE
KNOWN ACCOMPLICE: ELIZA
FAVOURITE PASTIME: SITTING ON CONSOLE IN THE BENTLEY

OWNER: MICHELLE NUGAN (PICTURED) | SHIH TZUS, 5 | **NUGAN ESTATE** GRIFFITH, NSW

PEPPIE

OBSESSIONS: DESIGNER CLOTHES AND GOGGLES
NAUGHTIEST DEED: STEALING SOCKS
PET HATES: BAD HAIRCUTS AND STUFFED DOGS
FAVOURITE TOY: STUFFED PUSSYCAT
FASTEST MEAL CONSUMED: GOURMET CHICKEN AND VEGIES
FAVOURITE PASTIME: WATCHING 'HARRY'S PRACTICE'

**TATLER WINES** LOVEDALE, NSW | MALTESE TERRIER, 2 | OWNERS: THEO AND FAY ISAK

TOBY

PET HATE: NO FOOD
FAVOURITE TOY: OLD SHOE
OBSESSIONS: FOOD, PATS, WATER, SLEEP
KNOWN ACCOMPLICE: BUDDY
NAUGHTIEST DEED: ATE A LARGE BAG OF CHOOK FOOD
FAVOURITE PASTIME: FOLLOWING GRAPE PICKERS TO EAT DROPPINGS

BUDDY

FAVOURITE TOY: BALL
KNOWN ACCOMPLICE: TOBY
PET HATES: CATS AND MAGPIES
OBSESSION: BALLS, WILL CHASE THEM ALL DAY
NAUGHTIEST DEED: JUMPING OUT OF THE UTE AT 50 KM/H
FAVOURITE PASTIME: CHASING BALLS

PET HATE: OTHER DOGS
FAVOURITE TOY: SOCKS
OBSESSIONS: BARKING AND EATING
NAUGHTIEST DEEDS: CHASING CARS AND LOSING HIS LEG
KNOWN ACCOMPLICE: PREVIOUSLY, BINNY HIS MUM
FAVOURITE PASTIME: SLEEPING WITH BOBBY THE CAT ON TOP OF HIM

**HOME KILN** ** NES** RANELAGH, TAS | *GOLDEN RETRIEVER, 16* | OWNERS: JULIE AND SEAN BENNETT

PET HATE: VISITS TO THE VET
FAVOURITE PASTIME: GREETING VISITORS
OBSESSION: GETTING ON THE END OF THE BED
NAUGHTIEST DEED: STALKING BLUE-TONGUE LIZARDS

FLEK

**CHARLIE BROWN**

FAVOURITE TOY: FRISBEE
OBSESSION: BEING THE LEADER OF THE PACK
NAUGHTIEST DEED: BOWLING OVER A GUY WHO WAS PLAYING FRISBEE
PET HATE: WHEN ANYONE ELSE HAS HIS FRISBEE
KNOWN ACCOMPLICES: TEXAS, BOOPH, MAYNARD AND DIRK

**PICARDY** PEMBERTON, WA | BULL TERRIER X, 10 | OWNER: ANDRIES MOSTERT

KNOWN ACCOMPLICE: ELLY
FAVOURITE PASTIME: SLEEPING
NAUGHTIEST DEED: STEALING A MARS BAR FROM THE LOCAL SHOP

# THE JOYS OF OWNING
# MAN'S BEST FRIEND
*by Mark Maxwell*

**after reading various dog books** *(with colour pictures), I decided I needed a dog that would be: 1) Intelligent; 2) Independent; 3) Have short hair; 4) Be fit and active to roam the vineyards; 5) Be attentive to cellar door visitors. Research led me to a German short-haired pointer or GSP for short – not to be confused with a GPS, which is used to find your location when lost. I left my GPS in the car one day and it was completely chewed by the GSP.*

*Molly, now nine, was the classic nightmare pup that ran away constantly and had me driving the streets of McLaren Vale beeping the horn and calling out for her, much to the chagrin of the neighbours. I thought the solution was to chain her up – but she ate through the post. I locked her in the chook pen, but she scaled the fence. Then I tried locking her in the winery but she chewed the control cable of a new Mono pump.*

*However after a few years she mellowed and became an obedient, understanding and generally pleasant companion. So to give her some company I acquired another GSP, Elly, thinking that I wouldn't have the same previous dilemmas. Alas, it was only weeks before computer cables were neatly sliced by sharp puppy teeth and tissue boxes were shredded to cover an area as large as a footy oval. The local birdlife got a hurry-up from Elly, a super-confident pooch who greeted all cellar door visitors.*

*But like fine wine, this breed matures with age, so now we have two mutts who are affectionate, intelligent and often obedient, who love people, food and adventure but not necessarily in that order.*

MARK MAXWELL IS CHIEF EXECUTIVE AND WINEMAKER AT MAXWELL WINES, McLAREN VALE, SA.

**JEN**

OBSESSION: *KEEPING AN EYE ON MOG*
PET HATE: *ABSOLUTELY FRIGHTENED OF SHEEP*
FASTEST MEAL CONSUMED: *SCHMACKOS*
KNOWN ACCOMPLICE: *MOG*

| **MILFORD VINEYARD** CAMBRIDGE, TAS | KELPIE X, 8 | OWNERS: CHARLIE AND ROBYN LEWIS

**CRUMPET**

OBSESSIONS: KANGAROOS AND FOOD
NAUGHTIEST DEED: EATING THE CAT'S DINNER
PET HATE: ORDINARY FOOD
KNOWN ACCOMPLICES: BILLY AND BLUEY
FAVOURITE PASTIME: RIDING IN THE CAR

**MOLLY**

OBSESSION: BEING PATTED FIRST
NAUGHTIEST DEED: EATING AN EXPENSIVE PAIR OF SHOES
PET HATE: LOUD NOISES
FAVOURITE TOY: WOOLLY BEAR
FASTEST MEAL CONSUMED: ROAST CHICKEN
KNOWN ACCOMPLICE: MILLIE
FAVOURITE PASTIME: CHASING STICKS IN THE VINEYARD AND DAM

**THISTLE HILL VINEYARD** MUDGEE, NSW | LABRADOODLE, 1 | OWNER: LESLEY ROBERTSON

FAVOURITE PASTIME: GRABBING STICKS FROM MOLLY
OBSESSIONS: WRESTLING WITH MOLLY, CHASING THE CAT
NAUGHTIEST DEED: CHEWING THROUGH A WINERY HOSE
PET HATES: LOUD NOISES AND FINISHING HER BONE
FAVOURITE TOY: MOLLY'S WOOLLEN BEAR
FASTEST MEAL CONSUMED: FILLET STEAK
KNOWN ACCOMPLICE: MOLLY

MILLIE

OWNER: LESLEY ROBERTSON | LABRADOODLE, 1 (LEFT) | **THISTLE HILL VINEYARD** MUDGEE, NSW

TESSA

FAVOURITE TOY: HER DOONA
KNOWN ACCOMPLICE: MOLLY
OBSESSION: BLACKBIRDS UNDER THE NETS DURING VINTAGE
NAUGHTIEST DEED: DESTROYING A SPRINKLER SYSTEM
PET HATE: THE GERMAN SHEPHERDS NEXT DOOR
FAVOURITE PASTIME: PERFORMING THE TASTE-TEST AT VINTAGE

**MAIN RIDGE ESTATE** RED HILL, VIC | GOLDEN RETRIEVER, 8 | OWNERS: NAT AND ROSALIE WHITE

FAVOURITE ACTIVITY: SWIMMING IN THE WINERY DAM
FASTEST MEAL CONSUMED: LOIN OF PORK FROM THE KITCHEN TABLE
OBSESSION: WAITING FOR HIS DAILY PIE FROM THE BOTTLING LINE STAFF

OBSESSION: BEING AROUND PEOPLE
NAUGHTIEST DEED: SWIMMING IN PUTRID WATER
PET HATES: THUNDERSTORMS AND LIGHTNING
FAVOURITE PASTIME: ACTING – STAR OF 'PETER PAN' MOVIE

JOE

228    KEVIN SOBELS WINES POKOLBIN, NSW | ST. BERNARD 6 | OWNERS: KEVIN, MARGARET AND JASON SOBELS

KNOWN ACCOMPLICES:
BEAUX AND TILLY
PET HATE: BEING LEFT OUTSIDE
FAVOURITE TOY: SMALL DOGS
NAUGHTIEST DEED: EATING THE
SCREEN DOOR AND CAT FLAP

XENA

SHIRAZ

OBSESSIONS: CHASING ANYTHING, SWIMMING AND GETTING A PAT
NAUGHTIEST DEED: EATING LARA AND MARGAUX'S DINNERS
PET HATE: BEING SENT OUT OF THE HOUSE
FAVOURITE TOY: TENNIS BALL
FASTEST MEAL CONSUMED: BEEF BURGUNDY PIE WITH SHIRAZ SAUCE
KNOWN ACCOMPLICES: LARA AND MARGAUX
FAVOURITE PASTIME: MEETING UP WITH OTHER DOGS

**TAYLORS WINES** AUBURN, SA | HUNGARIAN VIZSLA, 3 | OWNERS: THE TAYLOR FAMILY

OBSESSION: EATING
PET HATE: HOT AIR BALLOONS
FAVOURITE TOY: TOYOTA CRUISER TO SLEEP IN
FAVOURITE PASTIMES: CHASING MAGPIES, GOING SHOPPING
NAUGHTIEST DEED: RUNNING AWAY FROM HOME REGULARLY

CHLOE

POPPY

PET HATES: THE VACUUM CLEANER
AND THE TRACTOR

FAVOURITE TOY: DI'S SLIPPERS

KNOWN ACCOMPLICES: DRUCILLA, BELLA,
WISHBONE AND GEORGIA

FAVOURITE PASTIMES: RUNNING, EATING
AND SLEEPING IN THE SUN

**poppy**  *Faster than a '56 FJ Holden ... Able to leap vine trellises in a single bound ... More beautiful than a bubbling burgundy ... Is it a rare wild bilby on steroids? No ... it's Poppy, the whippet!*

*When visiting Blue Wren Wines at Mudgee, you may be lucky enough to spot the gorgeous Poppy. If you don't see her, look for that bolt of lightning on the horizon. It's most probably Poppy, clocking 60 km/h in a leisurely stroll amongst the vines.  A true pleasure to witness and a great test for one's eyesight.*

LUCY

OBSESSION: FOOD
PET HATE: BICYCLE RIDERS
FAVOURITE TOY: OSCAR
KNOWN ACCOMPLICES: OSCAR AND THE CHOOKS
FAVOURITE PASTIMES: SLEEPING AND EATING

**HERITAGE WINES** MARANANGA, SA | LABRADOR, 13 | OWNER: STEVE HOFF

FAVOURITE TOY: OWNER'S MIND
KNOWN ACCOMPLICES: MAX AND EG
PET HATE: COMING WHEN HE IS CALLED
FASTEST MEAL CONSUMED: CHUNKY STEAK
FAVOURITE PASTIME: WATCHING 'DOCTOR WHO'
NAUGHTIEST DEED: DUMPING ON THE
BACK SEAT OF THE STATION WAGON
FAVOURITE SONG: 'DON'T FENCE ME IN' BY BING CROSBY

**MUSTY**

**NICKY**

OBSESSION: FOLLOWING THE GRAPE HARVESTER
NAUGHTIEST DEED: HITTING ABI IN THE FACE WITH HIS TAIL
PET HATES: BEING KEPT INSIDE AND BOW WOW
FASTEST MEAL CONSUMED: BACON AND BADGER'S BONES
FAVOURITE PASTIME: HANGING AROUND THE SHEDS

OBSESSIONS: STICKS AND BLOW HEATERS
NAUGHTIEST DEED: UPROOTING FLOWER POTS
PET HATES: MAGPIES AND BEING WASHED
FAVOURITE TOYS: SOCKS AND LONG STICKS
FASTEST MEAL CONSUMED: BUTTERED BREAD
KNOWN ACCOMPLICES: PORTIA AND GABBY
FAVOURITE PASTIMES: CHASING STICKS AND BALLS

MALO

**DIRK**

PET HATE: STRANGERS
OBSESSION: LIVING THE LIFE
NAUGHTIEST DEED: NIPPING THE DELIVERY GUYS
FASTEST MEAL CONSUMED: CHICKEN NECKS
KNOWN ACCOMPLICE: BULA
FAVOURITE PASTIME: RIDING IN THE CAR

**BROKENWOOD WINES** POKOLBIN, NSW | AUSTRALIAN CATTLE DOG, 1 | OWNER: ELIAS RIGGS

OBSESSIONS: CHASING COWS AND BEING ALOOF
NAUGHTIEST DEED: SWIMMING IN THE DAM
PET HATE: DIRK
FAVOURITE TOYS: DIRK OR A RUGBY BALL
KNOWN ACCOMPLICE: MAYNARD
FASTEST MEAL CONSUMED: ANY RED MEAT ACCOMPANIED BY A GLASS OF CHIANTI

*"The noblest dog of all is the hot dog:*
*it feeds the hand that bites it."*

────── LAURENCE J. PETER

# TOMI: SHE'S A GRAPE DOG
*by Tessa Nicholson*

**Forget all that new-fangled** *equipment used in vineyards. All you need to tell whether or not it's time to harvest is Tomi the golden labrador.*

*She's five, extremely rotund, loves licking and is capable of picking a ripe chardonnay grape with just a sniff of her nose. To say nothing of a sauvignon blanc, pinot noir or gewurztraminer.*

*She even has her own vintage report in a wine magazine, with her nosy sniffs interpreted by her owner Ross Lawson, of Lawson's Dry Hills.*

*Tomi's penchant for vintage selection was discovered quite early on when, as a pup, she discovered some major advantages of living on a vineyard. Mr Lawson said he didn't realise she was feasting on the fruit until he noticed the grapes were missing from the lower branches of the vines.*

*"The first time I realised she was eating them was when I discovered there were whole rows for three or four bays without a bloody grape on them. She had been getting underneath the netting and eating them."*

*Her finely tuned taste developed even further when Mr Lawson was testing individual bunches for their sugar levels, before determining when to harvest.*

*Squeezing parts of a bunch onto the measuring equipment (a refractometer), he noticed Tomi licking the juice as it fell. Then when he threw the squeezed bunch onto the ground, he noticed Tomi only ever chomped up the bunches that were 22 brix or more (a brix is a measurement of sugar.)*

*Very selective, he thought, until he realised she was also only munching on bunches in the vineyard that had a high sugar level, over 22 brix.*

"The sugar level's got to be high and the acid level low before she'll touch them. I know that if I go into a vineyard and she races in and begins chomping, that the grapes are ripe and ready to harvest.

"She can do it on smell alone as well, she does it in the winery. She'll sniff the bunches and ignore, or sniff the bunches and eat. She's got as fat as a porpoise, though."

Tomi could be called a high-class sort of a dog, with chardonnay being her favourite, followed closely by gewurztraminer. And her fame is spreading, with the editor of the magazine Wine NZ dedicating a part of the vintage report especially to Tomi.

And what's more, she doesn't use phrases like 'toasted nuts, yeast, peach and rock melon aromas'. All Tomi does is give an appreciative slurp, which tells most wine drinkers all they need to know.

TESSA NICHOLSON IS A WRITER FOR *THE MARLBOROUGH EXPRESS*.

OBSESSION: ROSS LAWSON
PET HATE: HIGH-ACID CHARDONNAY GRAPES
FASTEST MEAL CONSUMED: 6 LB CHRISTMAS CAKE
NAUGHTIEST DEED: ATE CONTENTS OF THE PANTRY THREE TIMES
FAVOURITE PASTIME: GREETING PEOPLE AT THE CELLAR DOOR

TOMI

YOSHI

KNOWN ACCOMPLICE: WINDY
OBSESSION: DINNER, DINNER, DINNER
NAUGHTIEST DEEDS: REPEAT OFFENDER
PET HATE: THE RUSSIAN PROFESSOR

**VEGEMITE**

OBSESSION: STICKS

PET HATE: NON-WINE DRINKERS

FASTEST MEAL CONSUMED: THE ONE AFTER HE CHASED
ANDREW'S UTE HALFWAY TO BROKE (15 KM)

FAVOURITE TOY: HIS WOODEN 'CHATEAU MARGAUX' BOTTLE

KNOWN ACCOMPLICE: SPUNKY MARSH UNTIL HE WORE HER OUT

FAVOURITE PASTIMES: TELEVISION, SOCIALISING AND BARREL-ROLLING

NAUGHTIEST DEED: DRAGGING A DEAD KANGAROO THROUGH THE HOUSE

**MARSH ESTATE** POKOLBIN, NSW | KELPIE X, 13 | OWNERS: THE MARSH FAMILY

PET HATE: CATS
FAVOURITE TOY: BONES
FASTEST MEAL CONSUMED: PASTA
FAVOURITE PASTIME: EATING LEFTOVER GRAPES ON VINES
NAUGHTIEST DEED: PINCHING MOBILE PHONES OUT OF BACK POCKETS

SAMBA

TOBY

OBSESSION: *CHASING OTHER CREATURES*
PET HATE: *BEING IGNORED*
FAVOURITE TOY: *A BONE*
FASTEST MEAL CONSUMED: *FILLET STEAK*
KNOWN ACCOMPLICE: *GEORGE*
FAVOURITE PASTIME: *SUPERVISING THE WORKERS WITH GEORGE*

**TOBY**

248 | **DE BORTOLI WINES** BILBUL, NSW | JACK RUSSELL TERRIER, 4 | OWNER: DEEN DE BORTOLI (PICTURED)

**toby** *is a much-loved character at the De Bortoli*  *winery and well known for charming his way into the hearts of all visitors. Apart from his uncommissioned landscaping skills, he is also famous for being a bit of a lady's man/dog. The winery staff still recall the story of Toby's most famous escapade, which occurred during his lusty youth. He successfully overcame enormous obstacles to seduce a heavily guarded neighbourhood lady dog. With a grin and a twinkle of his eye, she was his.*

*Toby loves walking with his pet human almost as much as hanging with his best mate George, the spunky young German short-haired pointer. But it's the winery and vineyard that Toby loves best. Taste tester for Darren's stickys, exerciser for Deen, buddy for George, landscaper by day, lover by night ... where does he find the time?*

SUSIE

FAVOURITE TOY: ALBIE
PET HATES: POSSUMS AND WALLABIES
NAUGHTIEST DEED: STEALING ALBIE'S FOOD
OBSESSION: FOLLOWING THE WINEMAKER EVERYWHERE
KNOWN ACCOMPLICES: ALBIE AND BENNY THE WHITE CAT
FASTEST MEAL CONSUMED: ALBIE'S MEALS AND SMOKED SALMON
FAVOURITE PASTIME: SHOWING PEOPLE TO THE CELLAR DOOR

HARTZVIEW VINEYARD GARDNERS BAY, TAS | BORDER COLLIE X, 5 | OWNER: BOB PATTERSON

ALBIE

**COOPER**

FAVOURITE TOY: PEOPLE
OBSESSIONS: STICKS AND BALLS
NAUGHTIEST DEED: DRINKING BEST MATE'S COOPERS DRAUGHT
FASTEST MEAL CONSUMED: SHANE'S HAMBURGER
KNOWN ACCOMPLICE: ROSIE
FAVOURITE PASTIME: EATING OTHER DOGS' FOOD

| **CARDINGHAM ESTATE** CLARE, SA | KELPIE, 5 | OWNER: SHANE SMITH

FAVOURITE TOY: SOCKS
FAVOURITE PASTIME: SLEEPING
PET HATE: STAYING ON THE MAT
NAUGHTIEST DEED: NON-STOP BARKING AT THE DOOR

CHENIN

OWNER: GRAHAM UPSON | GOLDEN RETRIEVER, 4 | **SOMERSET HILL WINES** DENMARK, WA | 253

LARA

OBSESSION: FOOD
FAVOURITE TOY: KANGAROOS
KNOWN ACCOMPLICE: TOBY
NAUGHTIEST DEED: TUG OF WAR WITH A TIGER SNAKE
PET HATE: BEING LEFT OUT OF THINGS WHEN HER BROTHER IS AROUND
FAVOURITE PASTIME: WELCOMING VISITORS TO THE CELLAR DOOR WITH BROTHER TOBY

ELLENDER ESTATE GLENLYON, VIC | LABRADOR 8 | OWNERS: JENNY AND GRAHAM ELLENDER

FAVOURITE TOY: TREVOR THE CAT
KNOWN ACCOMPLICE: BLISS
NAUGHTIEST DEED: TRYING TO EAT A RED-BELLIED BLACK SNAKE
FAVOURITE PASTIME: CHASING ANYTHING THAT MOVES FAST

MOET

YOSHI

FAVOURITE TOY: THE BOOT
FASTEST MEAL CONSUMED: ANYTHING STOLEN FROM THE TABLE
FAVOURITE PASTIMES: EATING AND SLEEPING

PET HATE: LOUD NOISES
FAVOURITE TOY: TENNIS BALL
FAVOURITE PASTIME: SLEEPING
OBSESSION: HIS DOG BED AT THE FRONT DOOR
NAUGHTIEST DEED: DISMANTLED A KING-SIZED DOONA

ZEUS

**SQUID**

OBSESSION: RUNNING
FASTEST MEAL CONSUMED: BBQ SAUSAGES
KNOWN ACCOMPLICES: MIDGE AND ANGUS
FAVOURITE TOY: ANYTHING FROM ANGUS' TOY BOX
NAUGHTIEST DEED: RUNNING AWAY WITH A HANDBAG
FAVOURITE PASTIMES: SLEEPING IN THE SUN AND CHASING HARES IN THE VINEYARD

**LONGVIEW VINEYARD** MACCLESFIELD, SA | WHIPPET, 1 | OWNER: DUNCAN AND OOPY MACGILLIVRAY

JESSIE

PET HATE: CHILDREN
KNOWN ACCOMPLICES: BAILEY AND JIPPY
OBSESSION: BARKING AT THE ANGELUS BELL
NAUGHTIEST DEED: EATING SOMEONE ELSE'S BIRTHDAY CAKE
FAVOURITE PASTIME: LYING IN THE SUNNIEST SPOT
FASTEST MEAL CONSUMED: ANYTHING GOURMET

**WIRRA WIRRA** McLAREN VALE, SA | LABRADOODLE, 14 | OWNER: GREG TROTT

**jessie** *Over many years of visiting wineries around Australia, there was one dog that I remember most fondly. She was Wirra Wirra's adorable labradoodle, Jessie. This curly, black and most affectionate woofer had a fixation about people ringing the Angelus bell located at the winery. She would bark continuously from the time that they approached the rope until the last echoes faded.*

*I first met Jessie in the summer of 1997 and left Wirra Wirra that day thinking I would like to do a book on wine dogs (one of these days). It's taken six years for that day to arrive but unfortunately Jessie couldn't wait. Sadly, Jess passed away in early 2003, leaving everyone who knew her with warm memories of why the wine dog is such an important part of Australian wineries.*

*We miss ya, Jess.*

OBSESSIONS: SLEEPING AND EATING
PET HATE: PEOPLE IN BLACK PANTS
FAVOURITE TOY: THE CAT
FASTEST MEAL CONSUMED: BACON AND EGGS
KNOWN ACCOMPLICE: BARRY (RICHARD'S FATHER)
FAVOURITE PASTIME: SLEEPING IN THE OLD FORD UTE

**WELLS PARISH WINES** KANDOS, NSW | HUNGARIAN VIZSLA, 5 | OWNER: RICHARD TROUNSON (PICTURED)

# A GOOD IDEA AT THE TIME

*by Craig McGill*

**beware!** *If I hear one more person say, "You shouldn't work with animals or children" I may pounce on them and begin to gnaw off their leg.*

*The idea for this book originated over six years ago while Sue and I travelled through the wine districts of South Australia. Being avid dog lovers, we were pleasantly surprised by the huge number of woofers we came across. They came in all shapes and sizes and were always willing recipients of a good pat. (There was absolutely no sign of their darker side on this visit.) So an idea for a book was born from this love of wine and dogs. Was this a valid idea or some lunatic raving from a couple of loons who were enjoying their wine a little too much? No, what a silly thought. How can you enjoy wine too much? We had to do this book. The dogs of Aussie wineries demanded it!*

*So as I began to travel around Australia with my trusty photographer Justin, I told everyone I came across that I was writing a book on dogs in wineries. "You're mad!" was the most common response. But what was wrong with this idea? It was the first day of shooting (photography, not firing a weapon) when I found out the answer. I don't know how many times one can repeat the word 'sit' to a dog that obviously hadn't heard of the word before. Several hundred times and I lost count. It was a real test of patience that was wearing thin halfway through the first day. I reminded Justin that we only had 100 more dogs to photograph across four states. He quickly retorted that if a dog didn't maul me by the end of this job then he would. I didn't take my eyes off him for the next six weeks.*

Unfortunately, it was only a few days into the shoot before our first canine friend set upon us. Within a flash, Justin's jeans were ripped and the culprit left a perfect dental impression on my stomach. Ouch! We just looked at each other and thought, "What the hell have we got ourselves into?" But a deeper question beckoned. Will I return home only loving wine?

After several days on the road, we had already smelt like dogs, now it was time to think like them. We survived by becoming dog psychologists. This was the turning point. They warmed to us and we won them over (a constant supply of Schmackos helped). We were welcomed with open paws wherever we went. It was like they all knew we had a bootfull of dog treats. They got what they wanted and so did we.

In the end, over 100 dogs were photographed in seven weeks. There were a few casualties along the way (a chewed light meter, a watchstrap, and the occasional loss of dignity) but nothing really serious. And most importantly ... I returned with my love of dogs and wine firmly intact. Woof!

# O K, SO IT WAS A GREAT IDEA...

The first edition of Wine Dogs became a bestseller in Australia within six months of its release. What's truly amazing about this is that it was largely sold only at cellar doors. As Wine Dogs was independently published and distributed, only about twenty bookstores nationally sold Wine Dogs – so we were equally surprised by its success. Within weeks of its release, wineries from all around the world wanted their hounds to be Wine Dogs. Why isn't our woofer in your book? When are you doing Wine Dogs of Italy? Don't you know we have more winery dogs in Portugal than anywhere? Didn't you know we have the biggest, smartest dogs in the Napa Valley?

*Well to tell the truth, I didn't know the answer to any of these questions, so Sue and I thought the quickest way around these new dilemmas was to expand the reprinted edition and at least keep some of these nice people happy.*

*This time a number of photographers were used to expand the book. We also made sure we travelled to regions of Australia that weren't represented in the first edition. But by far, the biggest scoop for* Wine Dogs *was Kevin Judd's involvement. We are really happy to have Kevin photograph for us in New Zealand and his enthusiasm is no doubt reflected in the quality of the images within these pages. He's a true master of his craft. In fact, all the photographers in the* Wine Dogs *book are world-class photographers in their own right and it was an honour and absolute pleasure to work with them all.*

*Once again we met some wonderful people, played with some gorgeous puppies and drank some amazing wine. We hope everyone experiences some of the joy that we had in producing* Wine Dogs *... and remember life is too short to drink bad wine and owning a dog will make you live longer. What better way is there to drink more wine than by owning a woofer?*

# CRAIG McGILL
*Author/Publisher*

SHEPPARTON, NSW

ORIGINALLY FROM SHEPPARTON, VICTORIA, CRAIG IS A SELF-TAUGHT DESIGNER AND ILLUSTRATOR WHO STARTED HIS OWN DESIGN BUSINESS IN MELBOURNE AT 18 YEARS OF AGE. DURING THAT TIME HE WAS APPOINTED AS A DESIGN CONSULTANT TO THE RESERVE BANK OF AUSTRALIA.

HIS DESIGNS AND ILLUSTRATIONS HAVE GRACED BANKNOTES THROUGHOUT THE WORLD, INCLUDING THE AUSTRALIAN BICENTENARY TEN-DOLLAR NOTE. HIS WORK APPEARS ON THE ORIGINAL AUSTRALIAN $100 NOTE, PAPUA NEW GUINEA KINA, COOK ISLAND DOLLARS AND ENGLISH POUND TRAVELLER'S CHEQUES. CRAIG WAS ALSO INVOLVED IN THE DESIGN AND ILLUSTRATION OF MANY COUNTRIES' SECURITY DOCUMENTS SUCH AS PASSPORTS, BONDS AND TRAVELLER'S CHEQUES.

AT THE AGE OF 23 HE DESIGNED ALL OF THE COOK ISLAND BANKNOTES AND IT IS BELIEVED THAT HE WAS THE WORLD'S YOUNGEST DESIGNER TO DESIGN A COUNTRY'S COMPLETE CURRENCY. IN 1991, CRAIG MOVED TO SYDNEY WHERE HIS ILLUSTRATIONS WERE REGULARLY COMMISSIONED BY AGENCIES AND DESIGNERS BOTH IN AUSTRALIA AND AROUND THE WORLD.

HE IS NOW WIDELY KNOWN AS AUSTRALIA'S ONLY FREELANCE CURRENCY DESIGNER. MORE RECENTLY CRAIG HAS DESIGNED AND ILLUSTRATED FIVE STAMPS FOR AUSTRALIA POST.

CRAIG HAS BEEN CREATIVE DIRECTOR OF HIS OWN AGENCY, McGILL DESIGN GROUP, FOR OVER TWENTY-TWO YEARS. THE AGENCY HAS A DIVERSE, PROFESSIONAL BODY OF WORK WHICH COMBINES CRAIG'S TRADITIONAL, FINE ART STYLE WITH MORE 'MODERN' METHODS OF DESIGN.

*Tok, Craig and Tarka*

FAVOURITE FOOD: ROAST DUCK AND PINOT NOIR

FAVOURITE PASTIMES: VENTRILOQUISM AND DANCING WITH HUSKIES

NAUGHTIEST DEED: CHASING HUSKIES WHILE STARK NAKED

KNOWN ACCOMPLICES: SUE, TOK, TARKA AND STELLA

OBSESSIONS: BEER, WINE, LIFE AND TENNIS PLAYERS OF THE 1970s

PET HATES: INSINCERITY, STUPIDITY AND FOOLS

# SUSAN ELLIOTT
*Designer/Publisher*
*ALBURY, NSW*

SUSAN IS A MULTI-SKILLED ARTIST WITH A BACKGROUND IN FINE ART, ILLUSTRATION AND PRINTMAKING. AFTER COMPLETING TWO YEARS OF A PSYCHOLOGY DEGREE, SUE CHANGED TO A CAREER IN ART. SHE GRADUATED FROM THE CITY ART INSTITUTE IN 1986, MAJORING IN DRAWING, PRINTMAKING AND PAINTING.

AFTER TWO YEARS LIVING ABROAD, SUE RETURNED TO AUSTRALIA AND EXHIBITED HER GRAPHIC ART AND SCREENPRINTS EXTENSIVELY AROUND SYDNEY WHILE ALSO WORKING IN A NUMBER OF SMALL DESIGN STUDIOS. SHE HAS DEVELOPED INTO AN AWARD-WINNING GRAPHIC DESIGNER WITH OVER 15 YEARS OF EXPERIENCE IN THE INDUSTRY.

SUE JOINED McGILL DESIGN GROUP IN 1999 AS CO-OWNER AND CREATIVE DIRECTOR. HER INFLUENCE HAS CHANGED THE DIRECTION OF THE COMPANY BY CREATING A MORE VERSATILE AND DESIGN-FOCUSED AGENCY. SHE HAS BEEN RESPONSIBLE FOR THE DESIGN OF A NUMBER OF SUCCESSFUL PUBLICATIONS, WINE LABELS AND PRODUCT PACKAGING. SUE HAS ALSO DESIGNED AND DEVELOPED CORPORATE IDENTITIES AND LOGOS FOR AUSTRALIAN AND INTERNATIONAL CLIENTS.

*Stella and Sue*

*FAVOURITE FOOD: NOODLES*
*FAVOURITE PASTIME: WATCHING MOVIES WITH STELLA*
*NAUGHTIEST DEED: TEASING HUSKIES*
*KNOWN ACCOMPLICES: CRAIG, TOK, TARKA AND STELLA*
*OBSESSIONS: BATH SALTS AND THE TED MULRY GANG*
*PET HATE: WHISTLING*

# McGILL DESIGN GROUP

McGILL DESIGN GROUP WAS FORMED IN 1981 AND SPECIALISES IN PROVIDING A WIDE RANGE OF QUALITY GRAPHIC DESIGN SERVICES. THE STUDIO HAS PRODUCED NUMEROUS FINE WINE LABELS AND PACKAGING AS WELL AS CORPORATE IDENTITIES, ADVERTISING, PUBLICATIONS AND TELEVISION COMMERCIALS. www.mcgilldesigngroup.com

# PHOTOGRAPHERS

Harvey McMaster

**JUSTIN McMASTER** IS AN ACCOMPLISHED, SYDNEY-BASED, COMMERCIAL PHOTOGRAPHER. WORKING WITH WIDELY VARYING STYLE AND SUBJECT MATTER, HE INSTILS EMOTION INTO HIS IMAGES TO CREATE A UNIQUE VISUAL LANGUAGE. JUSTIN'S ENTHUSIASM, SKILL AND PATIENCE ARE EVIDENT WITH HIS OUTSTANDING PHOTOGRAPHS FOR *WINE DOGS*. ONLY ONE PAIR OF DESIGNER JEANS WERE MAULED IN THE SEVEN WEEKS JUSTIN PHOTOGRAPHED FOR *WINE DOGS*. www.justinmcmaster.com.au

*Pages 1, 7, 10, 11, 13, 18, 19, 22, 23, 30, 31, 42, 43, 44, 46, 47, 50, 62, 63, 65, 70, 71, 76, 77, 80, 81, 84, 85, 88, 89, 90, 96, 97, 98, 104, 106, 107, 111, 114, 115, 116, 118, 119, 122, 123, 125, 126, 127, 132, 133, 144, 145, 150, 151, 152, 153, 154, 155, 156, 157, 158, 159, 160, 161, 164, 165, 166, 168, 178, 181, 182, 183, 184, 192, 193, 198, 199, 204, 205, 208, 212, 213, 214, 215, 220, 223, 224, 225, 228, 229, 230, 231, 232, 234, 235, 236, 237, 238, 239, 245, 247, 248, 252, 253, 254, 255, 257, 258, 259, 262, 266, 267.* ALL IMAGES © JUSTIN McMASTER

Rover Judd

**KEVIN JUDD** IS CHIEF WINEMAKER AT CLOUDY BAY, NEW ZEALAND. HE HAS BEEN RESPONSIBLE FOR THE DEVELOPMENT OF CLOUDY BAY'S RANGE OF PREMIUM WINES SINCE ITS INCEPTION IN 1985. KEVIN HAS ALSO BEEN RECOGNISED AS ONE OF THE WORLD'S GREAT WINE PHOTOGRAPHERS. KEVIN'S BRILLIANT VINEYARD LANDSCAPES HAVE APPEARED IN NUMEROUS PUBLICATIONS AROUND THE WORLD. HIS FIRST BOOK, *THE COLOUR OF WINE*, WAS PUBLISHED IN 1999 TO MUCH CRITICAL ACCLAIM. NOW KEVIN'S PHOTOGRAPHS FOR *WINE DOGS* ARGUE A CASE FOR HIM BEING CONSIDERED ONE OF THE WORLD'S GREAT DOG PHOTOGRAPHERS. AFTER PHOTOGRAPHING FOR *WINE DOGS* KEVIN HAS ONLY 9 FINGERS REMAINING. www.kevinjudd.co.nz

*Pages 9, 14, 15, 16, 17, 20, 21, 25, 32, 33, 35, 40, 41, 48, 49, 54, 60, 61, 67, 68, 91, 113, 134, 137, 138, 139, 162, 172, 173, 180, 202, 211, 227, 243, 286.* ALL IMAGES © KEVIN JUDD

Maisy Boddington

**JAMES BODDINGTON** HAS OVER 18 YEARS EXPERIENCE AS A PROFESSIONAL PHOTOGRAPHER. HE IS RECOGNISED AS ONE OF AUSTRALIA'S LEADING PORTRAIT AND REPORTAGE PHOTOGRAPHERS. JAMES CONTINUES TO FREELANCE FOR AN EVER-INCREASING DIVERSITY OF EDITORIAL, CORPORATE AND ADVERTISING CLIENTS. HIS WORK FOR *WINE DOGS* SHOWCASES HIS NATURAL, HIGHLY CREATIVE AND UNIQUE COMPOSITIONS. JAMES ENTHUSIASTICALLY TRAVELLED AROUND VICTORIA WITHOUT BEING BITTEN ONCE!
www.jamesboddington.com

*Pages 24, 34, 38, 56, 58, 59, 72, 73, 82, 93, 108, 109, 140, 141, 146, 179, 194, 195, 200, 201, 206, 226* ALL IMAGES © JAMES BODDINGTON

Astro Clarke

**ALISTER CLARKE** IS CONSIDERED ONE OF AUSTRALIA'S LEADING ADVERTISING PHOTOGRAPHERS. COMING FROM A FINE ARTS BACKGROUND, ALISTER HAS OVER 20 YEARS PHOTOGRAPHIC EXPERIENCE WORKING ACROSS FIVE CONTINENTS. HIS TECHNICAL PRECISION, EYE FOR DETAIL, SENSE OF COLOUR AND UNIQUE HUMOUR HAVE BEEN IN DEMAND FROM CREATIVES WORLDWIDE. ALISTER PHOTOGRAPHED FOR *WINE DOGS* IN TASMANIA, CREATING SOME OF THE BOOK'S MORE UNIQUE-LOOKING PHOTOS. WHEN ON THE ROAD FOR *WINE DOGS*, HE WOULD ONLY EAT BONES AND REQUESTED HIS MINERAL WATER TO BE IN A BOWL. (*WINE DOGS'* ATTEMPTS TO PAY HIM IN BONES LED TO LOUD GROWLS.)
www.alisterclarke.com

*Pages 28, 29, 45, 64, 78, 79, 87, 94, 95, 110, 124, 167, 185, 196, 197, 216, 217, 250, 251.*
ALL IMAGES © ALISTER CLARKE

# PHOTOGRAPHERS

Sauvignon Lander

**ADRIAN LANDER** SPECIALISES IN CREATIVE STILL-LIFE, WINE AND FOOD PHOTOGRAPHY. HIS WORK HAS APPEARED IN NUMEROUS AUSTRALIAN AND INTERNATIONAL ADVERTISING CAMPAIGNS, MAGAZINES, BOOKS AND PERSONAL EXHIBITIONS. ALTHOUGH ADRIAN IS A CAT LOVER, *WINE DOGS* HOLDS NO GRUDGES, AS WE ARE AN EQUAL OPPORTUNITY EMPLOYER. www.adrianlander.com.au

*Pages 36, 37, 53, 86, 218, 219.* ALL IMAGES © ADRIAN LANDER

Jacko Shepherd

**EMILY SHEPHERD** IS A COMMERCIAL PHOTO-GRAPHER LIVING AND WORKING IN THE HEART OF THE McLAREN VALE WINE REGION, SOUTH AUSTRALIA. HER PHOTOGRAPHIC CAREER BEGAN 12 YEARS AGO WHILE WORKING AS A SCIENTIFIC/RESEARCH PHOTOGRAPHER FOR THE UNIVERSITY OF ADELAIDE. EMILY'S STUDIO WAS FORMED IN 2001 AND OFFERS A COMPLETE RANGE OF PHOTOGRAPHIC SERVICES ... AND YES, EVEN DOG PORTRAITS! www.studio-e.com.au

*Pages 74, 112, 176, 177, 191.* ALL IMAGES © EMILY SHEPHERD

**Massimo Griffiths**

**SIMON GRIFFITHS** IS A MELBOURNE-BASED PHOTOGRAPHER SPECIALISING IN FOOD, WINE, GARDENS, INTERIORS AND NOW DOGS. HIS WORK APPEARS IN MANY MAGAZINES AND BOOKS INCLUDING THE CANINE MASTERPIECE *WALKING THE DOG IN ITALY*. SIMON CAN OFTEN BE SPOTTED IN THE STREETS OF YARRAVILLE CHASING HIS WHIPPET, MASSIMO. www.labyrinth.net.au/~simong

*Pages 69, 120, 121, 130, 131.* ALL IMAGES © SIMON GRIFFITHS

**Tok McGill**

**CRAIG McGILL** www.realnasty.com.au

*Pages 8, 12, 26, 39, 55, 57, 66, 83, 92, 128, 142, 143, 149, 163, 174, 175, 203, 207, 222, 233, 240, 244, 246, 249, 256, 270.*

# ZOE CHARMS WIRRA WIRRA

### as with the choosing

*of the next Dalai Lama, the essential qualities for the Official Wirra Wirra Winery Dog were recognised at an early age in a pup brought to the cellars by winemaker Paul Carpenter. According to her master she is a three-month-old chocolate brown labrador.*

*He chose the name from memories of working in Beaujolais at Château de Bluizard. The Madame would shriek the name every morning at their dog who was expert at stealing toast off the breakfast table. Apart from the occasional calling card and indiscriminate chewing, Zoe has won most hearts, but we are waiting with interest to see her develop a true Wirra Wirra identity – excellent, exceptional and eccentric. Will she bark at the bell, appear magically at lunchtime, attempt to catch the boules at petanque like her predecessors? The possibilities are intriguing!*

STORY BY TONY BROOKS. TONY IS A WRITER AND PUBLICIST FOR WIRRA WIRRA, McLAREN VALE, SA.

# WINERY AND VINEYARD LISTINGS

## AUSTRALIA

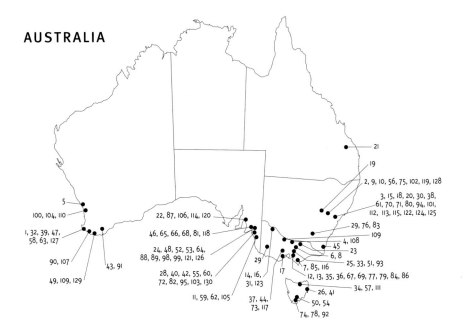

**1. Abbey Vale** PAGES 142, 207
392 Wildwood Rd, Yallingup WA 6282
Ph: (08) 9755 2121  Fax: (08) 9755 2286
Winemaker: Philip May
Cellar Door Hours: 10 – 5, 7 days

**2. Abercorn** PAGES 92, 106, 107, BACK COVER
Cassilis Rd, Mudgee NSW 2850
Ph: (02) 6373 3106  Fax: (02) 6373 3108
Winemaker: Tim Stevens
Cellar Door Hours: 10.30 – 4.30
    Thurs – Mon, 10.30 – 3 Sun

**3. Allandale Winery** PAGE 156
Lovedale Rd, Lovedale NSW 2320
Ph: (02) 4990 4526  Fax: (02) 4990 1714
Winemaker: Bill Sneddon
Cellar Door Hours: 9 – 5 Mon – Sat,
    10 – 5 Sun

**4. All Saints Estate** PAGE 165
All Saints Rd, Wahgunyah VIC 3687
Ph: (02) 6035 2222  Fax: (02) 6035 2200
Winemaker: Dan Crane
Cellar Door Hours: 9 – 5

**5. Aquila Estate** PAGE 155
85 Carabooda Rd, Carabooda WA 6033
Ph: (08) 9561 8166  Fax: (08) 9561 8177
Winemaker: Andrew Spencer-Wright
Cellar Door Hours: 11 – 5 Sat,
    Sun & Pub hols

**6. Barnadown Run** PAGES 36, 37
390 Cornella Rd, Toolleen VIC 3551
Ph: (03) 5433 6376  Fax: (03) 5433 6386
Winemaker: Andrew Millis
Cellar Door Hours: 10 – 5, 7 days

**7. Bass Phillip Wines** PAGES 179
Hunts Rd, Leongatha South VIC 3953
Ph: (03) 5664 3341  Fax: (03) 5664 3209
Winemaker: Phillip Jones
Cellar Door Hours: By appointment

**8. Bettio Wines** PAGE 13
Whitefield Rd, King Valley VIC 3678
Ph: (03) 5727 9308  Fax: (03) 5727 9344
Winemaker: Daniel Bettio
Cellar Door Hours: By appointment

**9. Bloodwood Wines** PAGES 86, 219
4 Griffin Rd, Orange NSW 2800
Ph: (02) 6362 5631  Fax: (02) 6361 1173
Winemaker: Stephen Doyle
Cellar Door Hours: By appointment

**10. Blue Wren Wines** PAGES 55, 203, 232, 233
433 Cassilis Rd, Mudgee NSW 2850
Ph: (02) 6372 6205  Fax: (02) 6372 6206
Winemaker: Drew Tuckwell
Cellar Door Hours: 10.30 – 4.30, 7 days

**11. Bowen Estate** PAGE 121
Riddoch Hwy, Coonawarra SA 5263
Ph: (08) 8737 2229  Fax: (08) 8737 2173
Winemakers: Doug & Emma Bowen
Cellar Door Hours: 10 – 5, 7 days

**12. Box Stallion** PAGES 194, 195
64 Tubbarubba Rd, Merricks North VIC 3926
Ph: (03) 5989 7444  Fax: (03) 5989 7688
Winemaker: Alex White
Cellar Door Hours: 11 – 5, 7 days

**13. Bristol Farm** PAGE 184
Bellingham Rd, Main Ridge VIC 3928
Ph: (03) 9830 1453  Fax: (03) 9888 6794
Winemaker: Under contract to
   Precision Wines
Cellar Door Hours: By appointment

**14. Brockville** PAGE 34
15th St, Irymple VIC 3498
Ph: (03) 5024 5143  Fax: (03) 5024 2818
Winemaker: Contract
Cellar Door Hours: By appointment

**15. Brokenwood Wines** PAGES 238, 239
McDonalds Rd, Pokolbin NSW 2320
Ph: (02) 4998 7559  Fax: (02) 4998 7893
Winemakers: Iain Riggs & PJ Charteris
Cellar Door Hours: 10 – 5, 7 days
   (except Christmas)

**16. Buronga Hill Winery** PAGE 108
Silver City Hwy, Buronga NSW 2739
Ph: (03) 5022 5100  Fax: (03) 5022 5135
Winemakers: Mal Stewart & David Cowburn
Cellar Door Hours: By appointment

**17. By Farr** PAGE 69
27 Madders Rd, Bannockburn VIC 3331
Ph: (03) 5281 1979  Fax: (03) 5281 1433
Winemaker: Gary Farr
Cellar Door Hours: By appointment

**18. Camyr Allyn Wines** PAGE 164
Allynbrook Rd, East Gresford NSW 2311
Ph: (02) 4938 9576  Fax: (02) 4938 9576
Winemakers: James Evers & Geoff Broadfield
Cellar Door Hours: 10 – 5, 7 days

**19. Canonbah Bridge** PAGES 204, 205
Merryanbone Station, Warren NSW 2824
Ph: (02) 6833 9966  Fax: (02) 6833 9980
Winemaker: John Hordern
Cellar Door Hours: By appointment

**20. Capercaillie Wine** PAGE 183
Londons Rd, Lovedale NSW 2325
Ph: (02) 4990 2904  Fax: (02) 4991 1886
Winemaker: Alasdair Sutherland
Cellar Door Hours: 9 – 5 Mon – Sat,
   10 – 5 Sun

**21. Captain's Paddock** PAGES 8, 57
18 Millers Rd, Kingaroy QLD 4610
Ph: (07) 4162 4534  Fax: (07) 4162 4502
Winemaker: Contract
Cellar Door Hours: 10 – 5, 7 days

**22. Cardinham Estate** PAGE 252
Main North Rd, Clare SA 5453
Ph: (08) 8842 1944  Fax: (08) 8842 1955
Winemakers: Stephen John & Emma Bowley
Cellar Door Hours: 10 – 5, 7 days

**23. Castagna Vineyard** PAGE 77
88 Ressom Lane, Beechworth VIC 3747
Ph: (03) 5728 2888  Fax: (03) 5728 2898
Winemaker: Julian Castagna
Cellar Door Hours: By appointment

**24. Charles Melton Wines** PAGE 76
Krondorf Rd, Tanunda SA 5352
Ph: (08) 8563 3606  Fax: (08) 8563 3422
Winemaker: Charlie Melton
Cellar Door Hours: 11 – 5, 7 days

**25. Coldstream Hills** PAGES 80, 93
31 Maddens Lane, Coldstream VIC 3770
Ph: (03) 5964 9410  Fax: (03) 5964 9389
Winemaker: Andrew Fleming
Cellar Door Hours: 10 – 5, 7 days

**26. Craigie Knowe Vineyard** PAGES 28, 29
80 Glen Gala Rd, Cranbrook TAS 7190
Ph: (03) 6257 8252  Fax: (03) 6257 8252
Winemaker: John Austwick
Cellar Door Hours: 9 – 5, 7 days

**27. Crawford River Wines** PAGES 120, 131
Upper Hotspur Rd, Condah VIC 3303
Ph: (03) 5578 2267  Fax: (03) 5578 2240
Winemakers: John & Belinda Thomson
Cellar Door Hours: By appointment

**28. d'Arenberg** PAGES 97, 98
Osborn Rd, McLaren Vale SA 5171
Ph: (08) 8323 8206  Fax: (08) 8323 8423
Winemaker: Chester Osborn
Cellar Door Hours: 8 – 5

**29. De Bortoli Wines** PAGES 248, 249
De Bortoli Rd, Bilbul NSW 2680
Ph: (02) 6966 0100  Fax: (02) 6966 0199
Winemaker: Darren De Bortoli
Cellar Door Hours: 9 – 5 Mon – Sat,
    9 – 4 Sun

**30. De Iuliis Wines** PAGE 255
Lot 21, Broke Rd, Pokolbin NSW 2325
Ph: (02) 4993 8000  Fax: (02) 4998 7168
Winemaker: Michael De Iuliis
Cellar Door Hours: 10 – 5, 7 days

**31. Deakin Estate** PAGE 24
Kulkyne Way, Iraak (via Red Cliffs) VIC 3494
Ph: (03) 5029 1666  Fax: (03) 5024 3316
Winemaker: Linda Jakubans
Cellar Door Hours: By appointment

**32. Devil's Lair** PAGES 104, 105, 245
Rocky Rd via Margaret River WA 6285
Ph: (08) 9757 7573  Fax: (08) 9757 7533
Winemaker: Stuart Pym

**33. Domaine Chandon** PAGES 14, 127, 227
'Green Point', Maroondah Hwy,
    Coldstream VIC 3770
Ph: (03) 9739 1110  Fax: (03) 9739 1157
Winemakers: Dr Tony Jordon
    & James Gosper
Cellar Door Hours: 10.30 – 4.30, 7 days

**34. East Arm Vineyard** PAGE 45
111 Archers Rd, Hillwood TAS 7252
Ph: (03) 6394 8466  Fax: (03) 6334 1405
Winemakers: Nicholas Butler
    & Bertel Sundstrup
Cellar Door Hours: 10 – 4 Sat – Sun/
    Pub hols, closed in winter

**35. Eldridge Estate** PAGES 72, 73
120 Arthurs Seat Rd, Red Hill VIC 3937
Ph: (03) 5989 2644   Fax: (03) 5989 2089
Winemaker: David Lloyd
Cellar Door Hours: 12 – 4 Mon – Fri,
    11 – 5 Sat – Sun


**36. Elgee Park Wines** PAGES 90, 223
Junction Rd, Merricks North VIC 3926
Ph: (03) 5989 7338   Fax: (03) 5989 7338
Winemakers: Tod Bexter
    & Kevin McCarthy


**37. Ellender Estate** PAGE 254
"Leura Glen" 260 Green Gully Rd,
    Glenlyon VIC 3461
Ph: (03) 5348 7785   Fax: (03) 5348 4077
Winemaker: Graham Ellender
Cellar Door Hours: 11 – 5 Sat – Sun/Pub hols


**38. Ernest Hill Wines** PAGES 244, 256
Wine Country Drive, Nulkaba NSW 2325
Ph: (02) 4991 4418   Fax: (02) 4991 7724
Winemaker: Chris Cameron
Cellar Door Hours: 10 – 5, 7 days


**39. Fermoy Estate** PAGE 126
Metricup Rd, Willyabrup WA 6284
Ph: (08) 9755 6285   Fax: (08) 9755 6251
Winemaker: Michael Kelly
Cellar Door Hours: 11 – 4.30


**40. Fox Creek Wines** PAGES 70, 71
Malpas Rd, Willunga SA 5172
Ph: (08) 8556 2403   Fax: (08) 8556 2104
Winemakers: Dan Hills &
    Tony Walker
Cellar Door Hours: 10 – 5, 7 days


**41. Freycinet Vineyards** PAGES 87, 196
15919 Tasman Hwy, Bicheno  TAS 7215
Ph: (03) 6257 8574   Fax: (03) 6257 8454
Winemaker: Claudio Radenti
Cellar Door Hours: 9 – 5, 7 days


**42. Frog Island** PAGES 84, 85
Lot 101, Limestone Coast Rd,
    Mount Benson SA 5725
Ph: (08) 8768 5000   Fax: (08) 8768 5008
Winemaker: Sarah Squire
Cellar Door Hours: 10 – 5, 7 days
    (excl. Christmas Day & Good Friday)


**43. Gilbert Wines** PAGE 31
Albany Hwy, Kendenup WA 6323
Ph: (08) 9851 4028   Fax: (08) 9851 4021
Winemaker: Jim Gilbert
Cellar Door Hours: 10 – 5, 7 days


**44. Goona Warra** PAGES 46, 47
790 Sunbury Rd, Sunbury VIC 3429
Ph: (03) 9740 7766   Fax: (03) 9744 7648
Winemaker: Nick Bickford
Cellar Door Hours: 10 – 5 Sun – Fri,
    12 noon – 5 Sat


**45. Grevillea Estate Wines** PAGES 12, 212
Buckajo Rd, Bega NSW 2550
Ph: (02) 6492 3006   Fax:  (02) 6492 5330
Winemaker: Nicky Collins
Cellar Door Hours: 9 – 5, 7 days


**46. Hahndorf Hill Winery** PAGE 177
Lot 10, Pains Rd, Hahndorf SA 5245
Ph: (08) 8388 7512   Fax: (08) 8388 7618
Winemaker: Larry Jacobs
Cellar Door Hours: 10 – 5, 7 days

**47. Happs** PAGE 62
571 Commonage Rd, Dunsborough WA 6281
Ph: (08) 9755 3300   Fax: (08) 9755 3846
Winemaker: Mark Warren
Cellar Door Hours: 10 – 5

**48. Harbord Wines** PAGES 176, 191
Stockwell Rd, Stockwell SA 5355
Ph: (08) 8562 2598   Fax: (08) 8562 2598
Winemaker: Roger Harbord
Cellar Door Hours: By appointment

**49. Harewood Estate** PAGE 30
Scotsdale Rd, Denmark WA 6333
Ph: (08) 9840 9078   Fax: (08) 9840 9053
Winemaker: James Kellie
Cellar Door Hours: 10 – 4

**50. Hartzview Vineyard** PAGES 250, 251
70 Dillons Rd, Gardners Bay TAS 7112
Ph: (03) 6295 1623   Fax: (03) 6295 1723
Winemaker: Bob Patterson
Cellar Door Hours: 9 – 5, 7 days

**51. Henkell Wines** PAGE 10
Melba Hwy, Dixons Creek VIC 3775
Ph: (03) 5965 2016   Fax: (03) 5965 2016
Winemaker: Hans Henkell
Cellar Door Hours: 11 – 5 Thurs – Sun,
    11 – 9 Fri – Sat

**52. Henschke** PAGE 96
Henschke Rd, Keyneton SA 5353
Ph: (08) 8564 8223   Fax: (08) 8564 8294
Winemaker: Stephen Henschke
Cellar Door Hours: 9 – 4.30 Mon – Fri,
    9 – 12 noon Sat

**53. Heritage Wines** PAGE 234
106a Seppeltsfield Rd, Marananga SA 5355
Ph: (08) 8562 2880   Fax: (08) 8562 2692
Winemaker: Steve Hoff
Cellar Door Hours: 11 – 5, 7 days

**54. Home Hill Wines** PAGES 78, 110, 216
38 Nairn St, Ranelagh TAS 7109
Ph: (03) 6264 1200   Fax: (03) 6264 1069
Winemakers: Peter Dunbaran &
    Sean Bennett
Cellar Door Hours: 10 – 5, 7 days

**55. Hugh Hamilton Wines** PAGES 112, 178
McMurtrie Rd, McLaren Vale SA 5171
Ph: (08) 8323 8689   Fax: (08) 8323 9488
Winemaker: Hugh Hamilton
Cellar Door Hours: 10 – 5.30 Mon – Fri,
    11 – 5.30 Sat – Sun/Pub hols

**56. Ibis Wines** PAGE 237
239 Kearneys Drive, Orange NSW 2800
Ph: (02) 6362 3257   Fax: (02) 6362 3257
Winemaker: Phil Stevenson
Cellar Door Hours: 11 – 5 Sat – Sun/
    Pub hols; for other times ring first

**57. Iron Pot Bay Wines** PAGES 64, 217
766 Deviot Rd, Deviot TAS 7275
Ph: (03) 6394 7320   Fax: (03) 6394 7346
Winemaker: Roderick Cuthbert
Cellar Door Hours: 11 – 5 Thu – Sun,
    Sept – May. June – Aug by appointment

**58. Island Brook Estate** PAGE 81
Loc. 817, Bussell Hwy, Metricup WA 6280
Ph: (08) 9755 7501   Fax: (08) 9755 7008
Winemakers: Mark Lane & David Watson
Cellar Door Hours: 10 – 5

**59. Jamiesons Run Winery** PAGE 182
Riddoch Hwy, Coonawarra SA 5263
Ph: (08) 8736 3380   Fax: (08) 8736 3071
Winemakers: Andrew Hales &
    Sophie Hannah
Cellar Door Hours: 10 – 4.30 Mon – Fri,
    10 – 4 Sat – Sun

**60. Kay's Amery Winery** PAGE 201
Kay's Rd, McLaren Vale SA 5171
Ph: (08) 8323 8201   Fax: (08) 8323 9199
Winemaker: Colin Kay
Cellar Door Hours: 9 – 5 Mon – Fri,
    12 – 5 Sat – Sun/Pub hols

**61. Kevin Sobel Wines** PAGE 228
Cnr Broke & Halls Rds, Pokolbin NSW 2321
Ph: (02) 4998 7766   Fax: (02) 4998 7475
Winemakers: Kevin & Jason Sobels
Cellar Door Hours: 9 – 5.30, 7 days

**62. Leconfield** PAGE 193
Riddoch Hwy, Coonawarra SA 5263
Ph: (08) 8737 2326   Fax: (08) 8737 2285
Winemaker: Paul Gordon
Cellar Door Hours: 9 – 5 Mon – Fri, 10 – 4.30
    Sat – Sun/Pub hols

**63. Leeuwin Estate** PAGES 66, 143
Stevens Rd, Margaret River WA 6285
Ph: (08) 9759 0000   Fax: (08) 9759 0001
Winemaker: Robert Cartwright
Cellar Door Hours: 10 – 4.30, 7 days

**64. Leo Buring** PAGES 192, 235
Eden Valley/Clare Valley SA
Ph: 1300 651 650
Winemaker: Matthew Pick

**65. Longview Vineyard** PAGES 186, 258
Pound Rd, Macclesfield SA 5153
Ph: (08) 8388 9694   Fax: (08) 8388 9693
Winemaker: Martin Shaw
Cellar Door Hours: 11 – 5 Sun

**66. Magill Estate Winery** PAGE 7
Penfolds Rd, Magill SA 5072
Ph: (08) 8301 5400   Fax: (08) 8301 5559
Winemaker: Oliver Crawford
Cellar Door Hours: 10.30 – 4.30, 7 days

**67. Main Ridge Estate** PAGE 226
80 William Rd, Red Hill VIC 3937
Ph: (03) 5989 2686   Fax: (03) 5931 0000
Winemaker: Nat White
Cellar Door Hours: 12 – 4 Mon – Fri,
    12 – 5 Sat – Sun

**68. Malcolm Creek Vineyard** PAGE 198
Bonython Rd, Kersbrook SA 5231
Ph: (08) 8389 3235   Fax: (08) 8389 3235
Winemaker: Reg Tolley
Cellar Door Hours: 11 – 5 Sat – Sun/
    Pub hols or by appointment

**69. Mantons Creek** PAGES 56, 146
240 Tucks Rd, Main Ridge VIC 3928
Ph: (03) 5989 6264   Fax: (03) 5989 6348
Winemaker: Alex White
Cellar Door Hours: 11 – 5, 7 days

**70. Margan Family** PAGE 199
266 Hermitage Rd, Pokolbin NSW 2320
Ph: (02) 6574 7004   Fax: (02) 6574 7004
Winemaker: Andrew Margan
Cellar Door Hours: 10 – 5

**71. Marsh Estate** PAGE 246
Deasys Rd, Pokolbin NSW 2320
Ph: (02) 4998 7587   Fax: (02) 7998 7884
Winemaker: Andrew Marsh
Cellar Door Hours: 10 – 5, 7 days

**72. Maxwell Wines** PAGES I, II, 74, 220
Cnr Olivers & Chalk Hill Rds,
    McLaren Vale SA 5171
Ph: (08) 8323 8200   Fax: (08) 8323 8900
Winemaker: Mark Maxwell
Cellar Door Hours: 10 – 5, 7 days

**73. Maygars Hill** PAGE 159
Longwood Mansfield Rd & Hume Hwy,
   Longwood East VIC 3666
Ph: (03) 5798 5417  Fax: (03) 5798 5457
Winemaker: Sam Plunkett
Cellar Door Hours: By appointment

**74. Milford Vineyard** PAGES 79, 167, 222
1431 Tasman Hwy, Cambridge TAS 7170
Ph: 0417 130 516  Fax: (03) 6248 5076
Winemaker: Andrew Hood
Cellar Door Hours: By appointment

**75. Miramar Wines** PAGE 174
Henry Lawson Drive, Mudgee NSW 2850
Ph: (02) 6373 3874  Fax: (02) 6373 3854
Winemaker: Ian MacRae
Cellar Door Hours: 9 – 5, 7 days

**76. Miranda Wines** PAGE 257
57 Jondaryan Ave, Griffith NSW 2680
Ph: (02) 6960 3000  Fax: (02) 6962 6944
Winemaker: Gary Wall
Cellar Door Hours: 9 – 5, 7 days

**77. Montalto Vineyards** PAGE 206
33 Shoreham Rd, Red Hill South VIC 3937
Ph: (03) 5989 8412  Fax: (03) 5989 8417
Winemaker: Robin Brockett
Cellar Door Hours: 11 – 5, 7 days

**78. Moorilla Estate** PAGES 94, 95, 197
655 Main Rd, Berriedale TAS 7011
Ph: (03) 6277 9900  Fax: (03) 6249 4093
Winemaker: Michael Glover
Cellar Door Hours: 10 – 5, 7 days

**79. Moorooduc Estate** PAGE 140
501 Derril Rd, Moorooduc VIC 3933
Ph: (03) 5971 8506  Fax: (03) 5971 8550
Winemaker: Richard McIntyre
Cellar Door Hours: 11 – 5, 7 days

**80. Mount Broke Wines** PAGES 18, 19
'Harrowby', Adam's Peak Rd,
   Broke NSW 2330
Ph: (02) 6579 1314 or (02) 6579 1313
Fax: (02) 6579 1313
Winemaker: Monarch Winemaking Services
Cellar Door Hours: 11 – 4, 7 days

**81. Mt Lofty Ranges Vineyard**
PAGES 65, 160
Harris Rd, Lenswood SA 5240
Ph: (08) 8389 8339  Fax: (08) 8389 8349
Winemaker: Peter Leske
Cellar Door Hours: 11 – 5 Sat – Sun/Pub hols

**82. Noon Winery** PAGE 82
Rifle Range Rd, McLaren Vale SA 5171
Ph: (08) 8323 8290  Fax: (08) 8323 8290
Winemaker: Drew Noon
Cellar Door Hours: 10 – 5 weekends only

**83. Nugan Estate** PAGE 213
60 Banna Ave, Griffith NSW 2680
Ph: (02) 6962 1822  Fax: (02) 6962 6392
Winemaker: Darren Owers
Cellar Door Hours: 10.30 – 4, 7 days
   (except by appointment)

**84. Osborns Vineyard** PAGE 59
166 Foxeys Rd, Merricks North VIC 3926
Ph: (03) 5989 7417  Fax: (03) 5989 7510
Winemaker: Dr Richard McIntyre
Cellar Door Hours: 12 – 5, 7 days.
   Oct – July by appointment

**85. Paradise Enough Wines** PAGE 200
175 Stewart's Rd, Kongwak VIC 3951
Ph: (03) 5657 4241  Fax: (03) 5657 4436
Winemaker: John Bell
Cellar Door Hours: 10 – 5, Thur – Mon

**86. Paringa Estate** PAGE 58
44 Paringa Rd, Red Hill South VIC 3937
Ph: (03) 5989 2669   Fax: (03) 5931 0135
Winemaker: Lindsay McCall
Cellar Door Hours: 9 – 5, 7 days

**87. Penna Lane Wines** PAGE 153
Penna Lane, Penwortham SA 5453
Ph: (08) 8843 4364   Fax: (08) 8843 4349
Winemakers: Ray Klavins &
    Stephen Stafford-Brookes
Cellar Door Hours: 11 – 5 Thurs – Sun,
    incl. Pub hols

**88. Penfolds Wines** PAGES 88, 89
Tanunda Rd, Nuriootpa SA 5355
Ph: (08) 8568 9290   Fax: (08) 8568 9493
Winemakers: Peter Gago, Glenn James,
    Steve Lienert & Oliver Crawford
Cellar Door Hours: 10 – 5 Mon – Fri,
    11 – 5 Sat – Sun/Pub hols

**89. Peter Lehmann Wines** PAGE 44
Para Rd, Tanunda SA 5352
Ph: (08) 8563 2500   Fax: (08) 8563 3402
Winemaker: Peter Lehmann
Cellar Door Hours: 9.30 – 5 Mon – Fri,
    10.30 – 4.30 Sat – Sun/Pub hols

**90. Picardy** PAGE 218
Cnr Eastbrook Rd & Vasse Hwy,
    Pemberton WA 6260
Ph: (08) 9776 0036   Fax: (08) 9776 0245
Winemakers: Dan & Bill Pannell
Cellar Door Hours: By appointment

**91. Plantagenet Wines** PAGE 39
Albany Hwy, Mount Barker WA 6324
Ph: (08) 9851 2150   Fax: (08) 9851 1839
Winemaker: Richard Robson
Cellar Door Hours: 9 – 5, 7 days

**92. Puddleduck Vineyard** PAGES 185, 188
992 Richmond Rd, Richmond TAS 7025
Ph: (03) 6260 2301   Fax: (03) 6260 2301
Winemaker: Andrew Hood
Cellar Door Hours: 10 – 5, 7 days

**93. Punt Road** PAGES 111, 208
10 St Huberts Rd, Coldstream VIC 3770
Ph: (03) 9739 0666   Fax: (03) 9739 0633
Winemaker: Kate Goodman
Cellar Door Hours: 10 – 5

**94. Pyramid Hill** PAGES 236, 259
194 Martindale Rd, Denman NSW 2328
Ph: (02) 6547 2755   Fax: (02) 6547 2735
Winemaker: Jim Chatto
Cellar Door Hours: 9 – 5

**95. Ralph Fowler Wines** PAGE 114
Lot 101, Limestone Coast Rd,
    Mount Benson SA 5725
Ph: (08) 8768 5000   Fax: (08) 8768 5008
Winemaker: Ralph Fowler
Cellar Door Hours: 10 – 5, 7 days
    (excl Christmas Day & Good Friday)

**96. Rees Miller Estate** PAGE 115
5355 Goulburn Valley Hwy, Yea VIC 3717
Ph: (03) 5797 2101   Fax: (03) 5797 3276
Winemaker: David Miller
Cellar Door Hours: 10 – 5 Sat – Sun/Pub hols

**97. Ridgeback Wines** PAGE 122
20 Howards Rd, Panton Hill VIC 3759
Ph: (03) 9719 7687   Fax: (03) 9719 7667
Winemaker: Martin Williams
Cellar Door Hours: By appointment

**98. Rockford Wines** PAGES 118, 119
Krondorf Rd, Tanunda SA 5352
Ph: (08) 8563 2720   Fax: (08) 8563 3787
Winemakers: Robert O'Callaghan
   & Chris Ringland
Cellar Door Hours: 11 – 5 Mon – Sat

**99. Saltram Wine Estates** PAGE 150
Nuriootpa Rd, Angaston SA 5353
Ph: (08) 8564 3355   Fax: (08) 8564 3384
Winemaker: Nigel Dolan
Cellar Door Hours: 9 – 5 Mon – Fri,
   10 – 5 Sat–Sun/Pub hols

**100. Sandalford Wines** PAGE 63
3210 West Swan Rd, Caversham WA 6055
Ph: (08) 9374 9374   Fax: (08) 9274 2154
Winemaker: Paul Boulden
Cellar Door Hours: 10 – 5

**101. Scarborough** PAGE 231
Gillars Rd, Pokolbin NSW 2320
Ph: (02) 4998 7563   Fax: (02) 4998 7786
Winemaker: Ian Scarborough
Cellar Door Hours: 10 – 5, 7 days

**102. Secret Garden Wines** PAGE 175
251 Henry Lawson Drive, Mudgee NSW 2850
Ph: (02) 6373 3874   Fax: (02) 6373 3854
Winemaker: Ian MacRae
Cellar Door Hours: 9 – 5 Fri – Sun/Pub hols

**103. Shottesbrooke Vineyards** PAGE 123
1 Bagshaws Rd, McLaren Flat SA 5171
Ph: (08) 8383 0002   Fax: (08) 8383 0222
Winemakers: Nick Holmes &
   Hamish Maguire
Cellar Door Hours: 10 – 4.30 Mon – Fri,
   11 – 5 Sat – Sun/Pub hols

**104. Sittella** PAGE 247
100 Barrett St, Herne Hill WA 6056
Ph: (08) 9296 2600   Fax: (08) 9296 0237
Winemaker: John Griffiths
Cellar Door Hours: 11 – 4 Tues – Sun/Pub hols

**105. S Kidman Wines** PAGE 130
Riddoch Hwy, Coonawarra SA 5263
Ph: (08) 8736 5071   Fax: (08) 8736 5070
Winemaker: Clemence Haselgrove
Cellar Door Hours: 10 – 5, 7 days

**106. Skillogalee Wines** PAGE 151
Trevarrick Rd, Sevenhill,
   Clare Valley SA 5453
Ph: (08) 8843 4311   Fax: (08) 8843 4343
Winemaker: Dave Plamer
Cellar Door Hours: 10 – 5, 7 days

**107. Somerset Hill Wines** PAGE 253
891 McLeod Rd, Denmark WA 6333
Ph: (08) 9840 9388   Fax: (08) 9840 9394
Winemaker: Brendon Smith
Cellar Door Hours: 11 – 4, 7 days

**108. Stanton and Killeen** PAGE 152
Jacks Rd, Murray Valley Hwy,
   Rutherglen VIC 3685
Ph: (02) 6032 9457   Fax: (02) 6032 8018
Winemaker: Chris Killeen
Cellar Door Hours: 9 – 5 Mon – Sat,
   10 – 5 Sun

**109. Stevens Brook Estate** PAGE 109
620 High St, Echuca VIC 3564
Ph: (03) 5480 2005   Fax: (03) 5480 2004
Winemaker: Kim Hart
Cellar Door Hours: 10 – 6, 7 days

**110. Talijancich Wines** PAGE 154
26 Hyem Rd, Herne Hill WA 6056
Ph: (08) 9296 4289   Fax: (08) 9296 1762
Winemaker: James Talijancich
Cellar Door Hours: 11 – 5 Sun – Fri

**111. Tamar Ridge Wines** PAGE 124
Auburn Rd, Kayena TAS 7270
Ph: (03) 6394 1114   Fax: (03) 6394 1126
Winemaker: Michael Fogarty
Cellar Door Hours: 10 – 5, 7 days

**112. Tamburlaine Winery** PAGE 229
McDonalds Rd, Pokolbin NSW 2321
Ph: (02) 4998 7570   Fax: (02) 4998 7763
Chief winemaker: Mark Davidson
Cellar Door Hours: 9 – 5, 7 days

**113. Tatler Wines** PAGES 50, 214, 215
Lot 15, Lovedale Rd, Lovedale NSW 2325
Ph: (02) 4930 9139   Fax: (02) 4930 9145
Winemaker: Jim Chatto
Cellar Door Hours: 9 – 5

**114. Taylors Wines** PAGE 230
Taylors Rd, Auburn SA 5451
Ph: (08) 8849 2008   Fax: (08) 8849 2240
Winemaker: Mitchell Taylor
Cellar Door Hours: 9 – 5

**115. Tempus Two Wines** PAGE 116
Cnr Broke & McDonalds Rds,
  Pokolbin NSW 2320
Ph: (02) 4993 3999   Fax: (02) 4993 3988
Winemaker: Sarah-Kate Dineen
Cellar Door Hours: 9.30 – 6, 7 days

**116. The Gurdies Winery** PAGE 38
215 St Helier Rd, The Gurdies VIC 3984
Ph: (03) 5997 6208   Fax: (03) 5997 6511
Winemaker: Peter Kozik
Cellar Door Hours: 10 – 5, 7 days.
  10 – 6 during summer

**117. The Hanging Rock Winery** PAGE 181
88 Jim Rd, Newham VIC 3442
Ph: (03) 5427 0542   Fax: (03) 5427 0310
Winemaker: John Ellis
Cellar Door Hours: 10 – 5, 7 days

**118. The Lane Vineyards** PAGES 157, 158
Ravenswood Lane, Hahndorf SA 5245
Ph: (08) 8388 1250   Fax: (08) 8388 7233
Winemaker: John Edwards
Cellar Door Hours: By appointment

**119. Thistle Hill** PAGES 224, 225
74 McDonalds Rd, Mudgee NSW 2850
Ph: (02) 6373 3546   Fax: (02) 6373 3540
Winemaker: Lesley Robertson
Cellar Door Hours: 9.30 – 4.30, 7 days

**120. Tim Adams Wines** PAGES 144, 145
Warenda Rd, Clare SA 5453
Ph: (08) 8842 2429   Fax: (08) 8842 3550
Winemaker: Tim Adams
Cellar Door Hours: 10 – 5 Mon – Fri,
  11 – 5 Sat – Sun/Pub hols

**121. Torbreck** PAGE 161
Lot 51, Roennfeldt Rd, Marananga SA 5360
Ph: (08) 8562 4155   Fax: (08) 8562 4195
Winemakers: David Powell & Dan Standish
Cellar Door Hours: 10 – 6, 7 days

**122. Tower Estate** PAGES 22, 166, 168, COVER
Cnr Halls & Broke Rds, Pokolbin NSW 2320
Ph: (02) 4998 7989 or 1800 772 223
Fax: (02) 4998 7919
Winemaker: Dan Dineen
Cellar Door Hours: 10 – 5, 7 days

**123. Trentham Estate** PAGE 141
Sturt Hwy, Trentham Cliffs NSW 2738
Ph: (03) 5024 8888   Fax: (03) 5024 8800
Winemaker: Anthony Murphy
Cellar Door Hours: 9.30 – 5, 7 days

**124. Tyrrell's Vineyards** PAGES 42, 43
'Ashmans', Broke Rd, Pokolbin NSW 2320
Ph: (02) 4993 7000   Fax: (02) 4998 7868
   or (02) 4998 7723
Winemakers: Andrew Spinaze &
   Mark Richardson
Cellar Door Hours: 9 – 4.30 Mon – Sat

**125. Vinden Estate Wines** PAGE 125
17 Gillards Rd, Pokolbin NSW 2320
Ph: (02) 4998 7410   Fax: (02) 4998 7175
   or (02) 4998 7421
Winemaker: Guy Vinden
Cellar Door Hours: 10 – 5, 7 days

**126. Vinecrest Fine Barossa Wine**
PAGES 132, 133
Cnr Barossa Valley Way & Vine Valley Rd,
   Tanunda SA 5352
Ph: (08) 8563 0111   Fax: (08) 8563 0444
Winemaker: Mos Kaesler
Cellar Door Hours: 11 – 4 Fri – Mon

**127. Voyager Estate**
PAGES 26, 83, 128, 149, 163
Stevens Rd, Margaret River WA 6285
Ph: (08) 9385 3133   Fax: (08) 9383 4029
Winemaker: Cliff Royle
Cellar Door Hours: 10 – 5, 7 days

**128. Wells Parish Wines** PAGE 262
Sydney Rd, Kandos NSW 2848
Ph: (02) 6379 4168
Fax: (02) 6379 4036 or (02) 6379 4996
Winemaker: Philip Van Gent
Cellar Door Hours: By appointment

**129. West Cape Howe** PAGE 23
Lot 42, South Coast Hwy, Denmark
   WA 6333
Ph: (08) 9848 2959
Fax: (08) 9848 2903
Winemaker: Gavin Berry
Cellar Door Hours:  10 – 5, 7 days

**130. Wirra Wirra** PAGES 260, 272
McMurtrie Rd, McLaren Vale SA 5171
Ph: (08) 8323 8414   Fax: (08) 8323 8596
Winemakers: Samantha Connew, Tim James
   & Paul Carpenter
Cellar Door Hours: 10 – 5 Mon – Sat,
   11 – 5 Sun/Pub hols

# NEW ZEALAND

3, 15, 22

21

14

2, 4, 5, 6, 7, 8, 9, 10, 11,
13, 16, 18, 19, 20, 23

1, 12, 17

**1. Akaroa Harbour Wines**  PAGE 54
*"Sunny Brae" Vineyard, Akaroa  NZ*
*Ph: (03) 304 5870   Fax: (03) 304 5873*
*Winemaker: Kirk Bray*
*Cellar Door Hours: By appointment*

**2. Allan Scott Wines**  PAGE 9
*Jacksons Rd, Blenheim NZ*
*Ph: (03) 572 9054   Fax: (03) 572 9053*
*Winemaker: Josh Scott*
*Cellar Door Hours: 9 – 5, 7 days*

**3. Brightwater Vineyard**  PAGE 113
*546 Main Rd, Nelson NZ*
*Ph: (03) 544 1066   Fax: (03) 544 1065*
*Winemaker: Tony Southgate*
*Cellar Door Hours: 11 – 5, 7 days in summer*

**4. Cloudy Bay**  PAGES 17, 41, 49, 202
*Jacksons Rd, Blenheim NZ*
*Ph: (03) 520 9140   Fax: (03) 520 9040*
*Winemaker: Kevin Judd*
*Cellar Door Hours: 10 – 4.30, 7 days*

**5. Domaine Georges Michel**  PAGE 139
*56 Vintage Lane, Blenheim NZ*
*Ph: (03) 572 7230   Fax: (03) 572 7231*
*Winemakers: Guy Brac de la Perriere*
  *& Peter Saunders*
*Cellar Door Hours: 10.30 – 4.30, 7 days*

**6. Forrest Estate Winery**  PAGE 68
*19 Blicks Rd, Renwick NZ*
*Ph: (03) 572 9084   Fax: (03) 572 9086*
*Winemakers: John Forrest*
  *& Dave Knappstein*
*Cellar Door Hours: 10 – 4.30, 7 days*

**7. Fromm Winery**  PAGE 16
*Godfrey Rd, Blenheim NZ*
*Ph: (03) 572 9355   Fax: (03) 572 9366*
*Winemaker: Hatsch Kalberer*
*Cellar Door Hours:*
   *11 – 5, 7 days October to May.*
   *11 – 4 Fri, Sat and Sun June to September.*

**8. Herzog Winery**  PAGE 138
*81 Jeffries Road, Blenheim NZ*
*Ph: (03) 572 8770   Fax: (03) 572 8730*
*Winemaker: Hans Herzog*
*Cellar Door Hours: 10 – 4, 7 days*

**9. Hunter's Wines** PAGE 137
Rapaura Rd, Blenheim NZ
Ph: (03) 572 8489   Fax: (03) 572 8457
Winemaker: Gary Duke
Cellar Door Hours: 9.30 – 4.30, 7 days

**10. Jackson Estate** PAGES 172, 173
107 Jacksons Rd, Marlborough NZ
Ph: (03) 572 8287   Fax: (03) 572 9500
Winemaker: Mike Paterson
Cellar Door Hours: By appointment

**11. Lawson's Dry Hills** PAGES 242, 243
Alabama Rd, Blenheim NZ
Ph: (03) 578 7674   Fax: (03) 578 7603
Winemaker: Marcus Wright
Cellar Door Hours: 10 – 5, 7 days

**12. Mountford Vineyard** PAGE 91
434 Omihi Rd, Waipara NZ
Ph: (03) 314 6819   Fax: (03) 314 6820
Winemaker: CP Lin
Cellar Door Hours: By appointment

**13. Mudhouse Wines** PAGES 32, 67
197 Rapaura Rd, Renwick NZ
Ph: (03) 572 7170   Fax: (03) 572 7170
Winemaker: Allen Hedgman
Cellar Door Hours: 10 – 5, 7 days

**14. Murdoch James Estate** PAGE 180
Dry River Road, Martinborough NZ
Ph: (06) 306 9165   Fax: (06) 306 9120
Winemaker: James Walker
Cellar Door Hours: 11 – 5, 7 days

**15. Neudorf Vineyards** PAGE 20
Neudorf Rd, Upper Moutere, Nelson NZ
Ph: (03) 543 2643   Fax: (03) 543 2643
Winemaker: Tim Finn
Cellar Door Hours: 10.30 – 4.30, 7 days

**16. No. 1 Family Estate** PAGE 60
169 Rapaura Rd, Blenheim NZ
Ph: (03) 572 9876   Fax: (03) 572 9875
Winemaker: Daniel Le Brun
Cellar Door Hours: By appointment

**17. Pegasus Bay** PAGES 35, 48, 134
Stockgrove Rd, Amberley NZ
Ph: (03) 314 6869   Fax: (03) 314 6861
Winemakers: Matthew Donaldson
   & Lynnette Hudson
Cellar Door Hours: 10.30 – 5, 7 days

**18. Riverby Estate** PAGE 61
290 Jacksons Road, Blenheim NZ
Ph: (03) 572 8488   Fax: (03) 572 8488
Winemaker: John Forrest
Cellar Door Hours: By appointment

**19. Spy Valley Wines** PAGE 33
37 Lake Timara Rd, Blenheim NZ
Ph: (03) 572 9840   Fax: (03) 572 9830
Winemaker: Ant Mackenzie
Cellar Door Hours: 10 – 4, 7 days in summer.
   All other times Mon – Fri

**20. Staete Landt Vineyard** PAGE 211
275 Rapaura Rd, Blenheim NZ
Ph: (03) 572 9886   Fax: (03) 572 9887
Winemaker: Ruud Maasdam
Cellar Door Hours: By appointment

**21. Stonecroft** PAGES 15, 162
121 Mere Rd, Hastings NZ
Ph: (06) 879 9610   Fax: (06) 879 9610
Winemaker: Alan Limmer
Cellar Door Hours: Sat 11 – 5,
   Sun 11 – 4, when available.

**22. Waimea Estates** PAGES 21, 40
Appleby Hwy, Hope, Nelson NZ
Ph: (03) 544 6385   Fax: (03) 544 6385
Winemaker: Michael Brown
Cellar Door Hours: 10 – 5, 7 days

**23. Wither Hills Vineyards** PAGE 25
211 New Renwick Rd, Blenheim NZ
Ph: (03) 578 4038   Fax: (03) 578 4039
Winemakers: Brent Marris & Ben Glover
Cellar Door Hours: 10 – 4.30, 7 days

**THANK YOU:** *I would like to thank my partner Sue for co-producing and publishing this book with me. I have no doubt that it couldn't have happened without her help and constant encouragement, enabling me to pursue my never-ending and sometimes dubious ideas. Add to that her great book design, which has helped make the book the success it is. Thanks Sue!*

*Wine Dogs (Sue and Craig) would like to thank all the people associated with the production of this book and helping the project become a success.*

*To Huon Hooke for his generosity and friendship. To Patricia, Norm, Isobel and Jim for putting up with us and for their great dog-sitting skills. And special thanks to all the winery people and dogs that spent time with us and helped us along our travels. To all our contributors, Huon, Chester Osborn, Robert O'Callaghan, Phil Laing, Max Allen, Lisa McGuigan, Zar Brooks, Sarah Ashton, Mark Maxwell and Andrew Marsh for their time and great work. Thanks guys!*

*Special thanks to Justin McMaster for his vision, skill and enthusiasm. To our other photographers, Kevin Judd, James Boddington, Alister Clarke, Adrian Lander, Emily Shepherd and Simon Griffiths for their world-class photography. We think your photography has helped* Wine Dogs *become one of the world's great dog books.*

*Wine Dogs would like to thank their major sponsor, Pedigree, for their support and enthusiasm for the title. Big thanks also to Justin Monaghan at Masterfoods Petcare, Richard Hogan at ZooWines, Catherine Rendell, eagle-eyes Roy Hutton, Fiona McCarthy, the 'rock giant' Peter Herring, Jane Beard at Moss Wood, Eliza Brown at All Saints, Pam O'Donnell and Angela Clifford at Rockford, Sean Blocksidge at Voyager Estate, Boyd Wright at Leeuwin Estate, Dan Dineen, Tameiko Armstrong at Photo Technica, Patrick at Rozelle Framing, Joanna Rich, Harvi, Pam McMaster, Terry McMaster, Betty Burnett, Jock Burnett, George, Mildred, Robbie and Joep at Glitzi Gifts (Sydney's most spectacular and glamorous gift emporium).*

*To the dogs that bit me – I'll never forgive you!*

**FUTURE WINE DOGS:** *If your woofer missed out and would like to be included in future reprints of* Wine Dogs *please contact us at the address below.* Wine Dogs *will be continually updated and increased in volume, so don't miss out.* Wine Dogs, *PO Box 964, Rozelle NSW 2039 Australia. Email: info@winedogs.com.au or check out our website at www.winedogs.com*

WINE DOGS: DELUXE EDITION
THE DOGS OF AUSTRALASIAN WINERIES

ISBN 0-9580856-2-5

COPYRIGHT © McGILL DESIGN GROUP PTY LTD, FIRST EDITION 2004
**WINE DOGS ® IS A REGISTERED TRADEMARK**

DESIGNED BY SUSAN ELLIOTT, COPYRIGHT © McGILL DESIGN GROUP PTY LTD, 2004
ALL ILLUSTRATIONS COPYRIGHT © CRAIG McGILL, McGILL DESIGN GROUP PTY LTD, 2004
ALL TEXT NOT ATTRIBUTED, COPYRIGHT © CRAIG McGILL, McGILL DESIGN GROUP PTY LTD, 2004

PROOFREADING AND EDITING BY ROY HUTTON

PRINTED BY EVERBEST PRINTING CO LTD, CHINA

PUBLISHED BY McGILL DESIGN GROUP PTY LTD, PO BOX 964, ROZELLE NSW 2039 AUSTRALIA
TELEPHONE: (+612) 9555 5090  FACSIMILE: (+612) 9555 5985

OPINIONS EXPRESSED IN WINE DOGS ARE NOT NECESSARILY THOSE OF THE PUBLISHER.